H [illegible] REMOVE STAINS

CLAREMONT BOOKS

PENGUIN BOOKS

Published by the Penguin Group
Penguin Books Ltd, 27 Wrights Lane, London W8 5TZ, England
Penguin Books USA Inc., 375 Hudson Street, New York, New York 10014, USA
Penguin Books Australia Ltd, Ringwood, Victoria, Australia
Penguin Books Canada Ltd, 10 Alcorn Avenue, Toronto, Ontario, Canada M4V 3B2
Penguin Books (NZ) Ltd, 182–190 Wairau Road, Auckland 10, New Zealand

Penguin Books Ltd, Registered Offices: Harmondsworth, Middlesex, England

First published by Penguin Books Australia 1993
Published in Penguin Books 1994

This edition published by Claremont Books,
an imprint of Godfrey Cave Associates Limited,
42 Bloomsbury Street, London WC1B 3QJ,
under licence from Penguin Books Ltd, 1995

ISBN 1 85471 765 0

CONTENTS

Introduction vii

A–Z **1**

Conversion Tables 146

INTRODUCTION

The need to clean and care for a household is always with us. This A–Z guide is designed to help by providing answers to your questions about stain removal and cleaning, including information about 'green' alternatives to household chemicals. As well, this book offers handy hints for economical household practice and for streamlining all those tasks that seem to take more of your time than they should.

For successful stain removal, prompt action is important: the more quickly you deal with a stain, the more likely you are to be able to remove it simply. With most stains, try cold water (not hot) first, flushing the water through the material if possible – or mopping up as you go if the stain is on carpet. If this first step doesn't work, try the more extensive treatments outlined in this book.

Make sure that you know about the cleaners you use. Availability doesn't mean that a household substance is harmless, to you or to the environment; some do a good cleaning job but need to be used with respect and an awareness of their dangers, if at all. To help readers to be informed, descriptions of most of the common cleaning agents are included in this book. But, as a general rule, if you can safely eat it – for example, lemon juice, vinegar, bicarbonate of soda – it's environmentally kind as a cleaner.

Dispose of all chemicals carefully. Paint, turpentine, sump oil, paraffin and insecticides, for example, are all toxic and should not be poured down the drain. Inquire at your local council about a collection point.

Be conscious of our scarce resources. Don't use more than you must – for example, don't use kitchen paper or tissues when a cloth will do the job, and don't use new plastic bags when you can recycle old ones. Think twice about running a tap, and use small containers for soaking, mopping and hand-washing.

Let this book help you with clever use of resources – your own, and the environment's.

A

ABSORBENT CLOTHS

- Absorbent cloths can be applied quickly to fresh spills on carpets or fabrics, to mop up the moisture. Clean cloths, paper tissues, paper towels, blotting-paper and sponges are all effective.
- White cloths are handy because you can see as you go how much of the stain is coming off. Blot and reblot until all the excess dampness is absorbed. Don't rub, as this will spread the stain.
- Treat the residue of the spill according to the specific instructions for it.

ABSORBENT POWDERS

- Absorbent powders are effective on wet stains or on grease. Powdered starch, talcum powder, powdered chalk, cornflour or bran will all serve the purpose. Sprinkle the powder over the stain and, once it has absorbed the moisture and dried, brush or vacuum it off. Continue until no more is absorbed.
- See also SALT

ACETATE FABRICS

- Acetate is a silk-like man-made fabric, usually made from wood-pulp. It is machine-washable in most cases.

- Be careful not to attempt to remove stains with vinegar, acetone or methylated spirits, or the fabric may dissolve on you.

ACETIC ACID

- Pure acetic acid is available from chemists.
- Vinegar is an impure and dilute form of acetic acid; nevertheless, white vinegar is adequate for most household cleaning jobs.

ACETONE

- Acetone, available from chemists, is a nail-polish remover and a solvent for animal and vegetable oils; but whatever you do, don't use it on acetate fabrics or they will dissolve before your eyes. Try it for removing sticky-label adhesive.

ACIDS

- While acid may not stain a fabric it is likely to destroy it, so rinse at once with cold water. Then use ammonia or bicarbonate of soda dissolved in water to neutralize the spill. Rinse well.

ACRYLIC

- Acrylic is a by-product of oil refining and is often used in knitwear, sometimes in a mix with wool. Most acrylics are machine-washable, but follow the manufacturer's washing instructions.

ADHESIVE TAPE

- Soak **washable** articles or cover adhesive with a wet cloth and leave. Then rinse and wash as usual.
- Sponge **non-washable** articles with methylated spirits, white spirit or eucalyptus oil.

ADHESIVES

- Many adhesives have their own special solvent, so in an emergency ring the manufacturer for advice.
- For **balsa-wood glue**, use acetone or non-oily nail-polish remover. On acetates, use amyl acetate and not acetone.
- For **contact** (cellulose-based) **adhesives**, use acetone or non-oily nail-polish remover. On acetates, use amyl acetate and not acetone.
- Cyanoacrylates (for example, **super glue**) bond in seconds. This type of glue is activated by water, and water may help in dissolving it. Hold a damp cloth over the spot until it becomes unstuck. If eyelids or fingers become stuck, don't panic: a damp cottonwool ball held over the eye will unstick it. There is a product on the market for removing super glue. Just follow the instructions.
- **Epoxy resin** is a glue and a hardener mixed. Spills can be removed with methylated spirits before they set. Once they have hardened they cannot be removed.
- Water-soluble **glue** may come out in water. Briefly run **washable** articles under a cold tap. Then treat

with ammonia or soak in detergent. Rinse, then wash as usual. Sponge **non-washable** articles with cold water, treat with household ammonia, and sponge with cold water again.

- For **PVA** (polyvinyl acetate, filled PVA), dab articles with methylated spirits.
- Fresh **plastic glue** stains on **washable** articles can be removed by washing in detergent and warm water. Some dried stains can be removed if you boil the article in a solution of 10 per cent white vinegar in water for about 15 minutes. Then rinse and wash as usual.

ALCOHOL see BEER; WINE; SPIRITS

ALUMINIUM

- Wash aluminiumware in warm sudsy water and rub gently with fine steel wool. Rub in one direction only. To shine, use a soft cloth and some cloudy ammonia.
- If food burns on the bottom of an aluminium pan, cover it with vinegar and add 1 tablespoon of salt. Soak overnight and scrub the pan the following day.
- Coloured aluminium should not be washed in a dishwasher. Avoid bicarbonate of soda or washing soda when cleaning.

AMMONIA

- Household ammonia and cloudy ammonia (that's

ammonia with soap in it) are both made specifically for use around the house.

- Always use gloves when handling and don't use in an unventilated space as the fumes are very powerful.
- Ammonia can restore colour altered by contact with acids.
- Never use undiluted on:
  - wool or silk;
  - blended fabrics containing wool or silk;
  - aluminium.

AMYL ACETATE

- Amyl acetate, available from chemists, is a solvent for celluloid, cellulose paint and nail polish. It's flammable and toxic, so be careful when using: don't breathe in the fumes and keep the windows open.
- Amyl acetate can be used on acetate fabrics as long as the stain contains no acetone.

ANGORA

- Angora is the soft fluffy goat's wool used in jumpers, scarves and hats. It's sometimes mixed with wool or nylon. Treat as you would your best knitwear.

ANTI-PERSPIRANTS

∟ Dab with dry-cleaning fluid and then try ammonia. Rinse well.

ANTS

- Meat strongly attracts some ants: clean up all scraps. Jams, sugar and honey are best kept out of reach in the fridge, and you should rinse plates before putting them in the dishwasher or they'll move in there.
- If ants are a minor irritation, try putting talcum powder on their trails. Crushed garlic will also deter them.
- A mixture in equal proportions of borax and sugar, icing sugar or jam is a more permanent cure, although it does not take effect immediately. It is also poisonous to animals and humans, so keep it well out of reach on the ant trail.

APHIDS

- A repeated application of soapy water, onion or garlic spray, or white oil, are the 'green' ways to control aphids and thrip. Pyrethrum spray will also offer temporary control.
- To rid nappies of thrip after taking them off the clothes-line, put them in the tumble-dryer on HIGH for 5 minutes.

APPLE JUICE

- On **clothing**, sponge off apple juice immediately with cold water.
- On **carpet**, smother an apple-juice spill with salt and leave for several hours. Then vacuum. Try carpet shampoo on any remaining stain.

APPLES

- Tinned strained apple baby food is a short cut to apple sauce for your roast pork.

ARTIFICIAL FLOWERS

- Place grubby artificial flowers in a large paper bag, add lots of salt and shake vigorously. Then run water through the flowers and watch the dirt just wash away.

ASTRINGENT

- Apple cider vinegar in warm water splashed on to a clean face and left to dry is a good astringent.

AVOCADO

- There are 3 ways of ripening avocados:
  - wrap individually in dry newspaper or a brown-paper bag and leave in a warm dry place;
  - place in a brown-paper bag and tuck them up in a bed with the electric blanket turned on;
  - heat in the microwave for up to 2 minutes on LOW, turning once during heating time.
- Store ripe avocados in the vegetable section of the fridge.
- If you are storing half an avocado, leave the stone in.
- Avocado flesh discolours after peeling or slicing. Delay this with a squeeze of lemon juice.

B

BACON

- To stop bacon rashers curling as they are cooked, snip through the rind in several places, or remove rind altogether and save it to add to stock or for flavouring a casserole.
- Bacon freezes well. Separate the rashers before freezing, so that you can thaw only what you need.

BALLPOINT PEN

- On **non-acetate clothing**, dab the mark with methylated spirits, then rinse; or, if you have just made the mark, rub a little pure soap into it and scratch off as much as you can with a fingernail, then rinse. Send **acetates** to the dry-cleaner, with information about the fabric and the stain.
- On **vinyl**, spray with hair spray and rub gently.
- On **carpet**, use white spirit and rub gently.

BANANAS

- Make a treat for children by placing a banana on an ice-lolly stick and freezing it.
- To ripen bananas, place them in a paper bag with an apple.

BARBECUE

- To clean cooking plates more easily, sprinkle a handful of salt on the plate while still very hot and leave until it cools. If your barbecue is the type with a lid it is best cleaned just before you are about to use it: the grease from the previous barbecue protects the plates from rust, and the lid will hide the grease. Otherwise, oil the plates after washing.
- A teaspoon and a half of salt sprinkled on your barbecue fire will give you glowing coals.

BASIL

- Basil is a herb that bluebottles don't like: plant by a doorway.
- Intersperse basil with your tomato plants and you will have a home-grown pasta sauce at your back door.
- Use it fresh or dry in Italian dishes, and to season tomato dishes, peppers, aubergines and vegetable soup. Fresh leaves are an interesting addition to most salads.

BASIN

- Wipe over the bathroom basin with bicarbonate of soda on a damp cloth. Add to the shine by going over it with white vinegar on a cloth. Use an old toothbrush to clean the awkward bits around the base of the taps.

BATH

- To remove stains, rub with one of the following mixtures:
  - salt and turpentine;
  - salt and lemon juice;
  - bicarbonate of soda and lemon juice.

  Then rinse.
- If staining is severe, cover with a paste of cream of tartar and peroxide and leave for several hours before rinsing.

BATHROOM

- There is a lot to be said for the 'user pays' principle, which involves each household member in cleaning the bath and shower recess after use. This way the load is spread and the task never becomes arduous. A cloth kept within easy reach and a polite request to the user may work for your household.
- The bathroom won't steam up so much if you turn the cold tap on first, then add the hot water.

BAY LEAVES

- Fresh or dried bay leaves are used in marinades, stocks, soups, casseroles, poultry and fish dishes. Bay leaves make up one quarter of a bouquet garni, along with thyme, marjoram and parsley.
- Use a bay leaf as an anti-weevil device. Simply add

one to your storage jars of flour and cereal (you can tape it to the lid).

BEER

- Soak the stained garment in 1 litre (1¾ pints) of warm water to which 2 tablespoons of powdered borax has been added. Rinse well.

BEETROOT

- Rinse under the cold-water tap as soon as you can. Then work detergent into the stain with your finger and thumb and wash as usual.
- Alternatively, simply sponge with plain cold water or let cold water run briefly through the stained fabric.

BICARBONATE OF SODA

- The alkali bicarbonate of soda (also called sodium bicarbonate or sodium hydrogen carbonate) is a white crystalline or granular powder with many household uses. As a powder, it is useful for cleaning surfaces; dissolved in water, it will remove acidic stains, for example, fruit juice.

BIRD DROPPINGS

- Wipe off the deposit. Soak **washable** articles in warm detergent solution or treat with hydrogen peroxide. Rinse and wash as usual. Treat **non-washable** articles with diluted household ammonia and then with white vinegar. Sponge with cold water. Dry as quickly as possible.

BITUMEN see TAR

BLANKETS

- Store blankets in a large rubbish bag with a cake of soap so that they will be moth-free and sweet-smelling when needed.

BLEACHES

- Used in many household bleaches, **chlorine bleach** (sodium hypochlorite) has a distinctive and pungent smell. Always follow the manufacturer's instructions.
- If you use a chlorine bleach as a lavatory cleaner, do not use it in conjunction with other cleaners. **Chlorine** and **ammonia** used together react with one another, producing a poisonous gas.
- Old stains on fabrics can be bleached out, but remember to wear rubber gloves when using a bleach. Don't use chlorine bleaches undiluted, and don't use even diluted chlorine bleach on wool, rayon, silk, deep-coloured or drip-dry cottons or cottons with special finishes.
- **Hydrogen peroxide**, available from chemists, can be used on wool and silk.
- **Lemon juice** is a safe bleach you may have on hand when the laundry shelves are bare. A soaking in lemon

juice and water can often do the job a commercial bleach would do.

BLENDER

- To clean a blender, partly fill with hot water and add a drop of detergent. Cover and turn on for a few seconds. Rinse with hot water and drain dry.

BLOOD

- A fresh bloodstain on **clothing** can be rinsed out in cold salted water. Whatever you do, don't use hot water. Just add a teaspoon of salt to half a litre (¾ pint) of cold water and soak or sponge the stain as soon as possible.
- If the blood has dried, first brush off as much as possible. Then, either bleach with a drop of hydrogen peroxide; or cover with a paste of powdered borax and water, allow to dry, and brush off. Then wash or clean according to the instructions for the fabric.
- On **carpet**, apply cold water and blot with an absorbent cloth as many times as necessary.

BLUEBOTTLES

- Bluebottles do not like basil. Other herbs useful as insect repellents are mint, fennel, tansy, pennyroyal and feverfew.

BOIL-OVERS

- A lump of butter or a tablespoon of cooking oil added to the water will prevent rice, noodles or pasta from boiling over or sticking together.

BONE HANDLES see IVORY HANDLES

BORAX

- Borax, or sodium tetraborate, is an effective water-softener and antiseptic, and an essential ingredient in a stain-removing kit. It is available from supermarkets and hardware shops. It can be in the form of colourless crystalline salt, or white powder.

BOUQUET GARNI

- A bouquet garni is a small bunch of marjoram, parsley, thyme and bay leaf, often listed as an ingredient in casseroles, stews and soups. Commercial bouquets garnis come in little bags. Discard after use.

BRASS

- Commercial brass polish is probably the easiest and most efficient way to clean brass.
- A 'greener' way is to rub with a piece of lemon sprinkled with salt; rinse, dry, then rub with olive oil. Alternatively, make a paste of 2 parts white vinegar to 1 part salt; rub on and leave for 5 minutes; then rinse carefully and polish dry.

- To finish off (whatever method you have chosen) you can use a cloth dipped in dry plain flour. This removes all trace of polish and produces an excellent shine.

BREAD

- To freshen up yesterday's bread, put the loaf in a brown-paper bag or in foil, and put in a moderate oven to heat through. The loaf may be sprinkled with milk or water first.
- In the microwave, heat an average loaf on HIGH for 90 seconds (not longer!), just before serving.

BREAD BAGS

- Keep your sliced-bread bags and use them one-third filled with potting mix for seedlings and cuttings, or for making a mini-greenhouse over a pot or punnet.
- See also SLEEVE PROTECTORS.

BROCADE

- Don't attempt to hand-wash brocades; they are too heavy when wet. Dry-clean them instead.

BRUSHES

- Clean up synthetic bristles of brushes by soaking them in bleach.

BRUSSELS SPROUTS

- A cross-shaped cut into the base of Brussels sprouts ensures that they will cook evenly.

BUBBLE MIX

- To make a really tough bubble-blowing mix, you need 1 part each liquid detergent and glycerine to 5 parts water and a pinch of sugar. These bubbles really last.
- Two parts warm water to 1 part washing-up liquid and you have an ordinary bubble mix.

BUMPER STICKERS

- Nail-polish remover applied to an old bumper sticker will begin to loosen it. Then you can scrape it away with a blade scraper or a knife.

BURNS see CIGARETTE BURNS; SCORCH MARKS

BUTTER

- For butter on **upholstery**:
  1 scrape off as much as you can;
  2 iron with a warm iron between layers of absorbent paper, checking frequently to make sure that you don't damage the fabric.
- On **fabric**:
  1 remove excess;
  2 try washing in hot water using detergent;
  3 if the stain remains, dab with dry-cleaning fluid.

- To make cold butter easier to spread, try grating it first.

BUTTONS

- Before wearing a garment, dab the stitching underneath the buttons with a clear nail polish, to ensure that they will stay on.

C

CALAMINE LOTION

- Sponge articles with water, then with dry-cleaning fluid. Keep moist. Repeat if necessary. Then wash as usual.

CANDLE WAX

- On **non-washable** fabric, wait until the wax is dry, then scrape off as much as possible. Either cover with ice, or put in a plastic bag in the freezer for an hour or two. Then place fabric between sheets of blotting paper or brown paper and iron with a warm iron. Remove any remainder with methylated spirits or dry-cleaning fluid.
- If the fabric is **washable in hot water**, spread the stained segment of the fabric over a bowl or bucket and pour hot water on it from a height.

- If **candle-holders** are coated with wax, put them in the freezer for an hour or so. The wax will then peel off easily.

CANDLES

- Prevent candles dripping by placing them in the freezer for several hours before use.

CANE FURNITURE

- Sagging and grubby cane furniture can be cleaned and tightened by scrubbing it with hot salted water. Use a nail-brush and a toothbrush for the hard-to-reach areas. Place in the sun or in a well-ventilated area and allow it to dry. When it is thoroughly dry, apply either lemon oil or cedar oil to prevent cracking and splitting.

CANVAS SHOES

- Fabric protector sprayed on new canvas shoes will help keep them looking new.

CAR POLISH AND WAX

- Treat fabric with dry-cleaning fluid. Then work liquid detergent into the stain, from the back if possible. Rinse. Then wash as usual if the article is washable.

CARAMEL

- For **washable** fabrics, rinse first with cold water; then treat with liquid detergent. If the stain persists, treat with a solution of half hydrogen peroxide and half water. Then rinse and wash as usual. If the article is **non-washable**, sponge lightly with cold water.

CARBOLIC ACID

- Carbolic acid (phenol) is used in general disinfectants for cleaning floors, drains and toilets, and in timber preservatives.

CARBON

- Use methylated spirits to remove pencil carbon stains on clothing. For carbon typing paper, use Dettol instead of methylated spirits and lightly sponge off.

CARPET STAINS

- The golden rule for removing stains from carpet is to begin when the spill is still fresh. Mop up the excess moisture with an absorbent cloth or white paper towels. Douse the stain with warm water rather than hot water and be careful not to get the carpet too wet. Always mop up excess moisture and clean from the outside of the stain to the centre. Repeat this procedure until the mopping is not picking up any stain.
- If the stain is still visible, add a teaspoon of non-bleach laundry detergent (or wool mix – see WOOL MIX for recipe – if the carpet is pure wool) and a teaspoon of white vinegar to 1 litre (1¾ pints) of warm water and mop again. Leave for 5 minutes. Then rinse with

warm water, blotting the stain thoroughly. Repeat until you are confident you have removed all the detergent. Then remove all the moisture by blotting with white paper towels or cloths. Leave dry ones on the stain overnight, pressed down by a weight – but be careful to choose a weight that will not add another stain to the carpet.

- If you are unable to catch the stain while it is still fresh, see individual entries (for example, INK) for further advice.

CARPET SWEEPER

- Dampen the sweeper brushes before use and they will pick up dust and lint more effectively.

CAST IRON

- Cast-iron utensils should be tempered before use:
  1 wipe over with some cooking oil on a paper towel;
  2 sprinkle a little salt on the inside;
  3 allow to heat for about 5 minutes.
- Prevent rust by ensuring that the utensils are completely dry before putting away:
  1 wipe with a dry cloth;
  2 rub over the entire surface with a little oil.

CASTOR OIL

- Castor oil is a good leather conditioner.
- See also LEATHER LUGGAGE; LEATHER UPHOLSTERY; SHOES.

CAUSTIC SODA

- Caustic soda (sodium hydroxide) is a strong alkali used in the manufacture of soap, lavatory cleaners, oven cleaners and drain cleaners, and as a paint remover. It can be used as a last-resort cleaner for ovens and bad stains on baths and basins. As an oven cleaner it is available as a stick, a jelly and a liquid. In this form it will burn the skin, and may even penetrate rubber gloves, so handle it with extreme care if you feel you must use it at all.
- See also LYE.

CEMENT

- Soak cement-stained clothes in cold water with a tablespoon of salt and 250 ml (8 fl oz) of vinegar.

CERAMIC TILES

- Clean tiles with white vinegar or methylated spirits on a damp cloth.

CHAMOIS

- Wash in warm water to which a little household ammonia has been added. Do not use soap. Squeeze out the excess water. Store in the container it came in to ensure that it stays soft.

CHANDELIERS

- Without dismantling the chandelier, immerse each

pendant for a few seconds in a glass of hot water and vinegar, and allow to drip dry. Remember to place newspaper on the floor beneath to collect the drips.

CHEWING GUM

- On **fabric**:
  1. put the garment in a plastic bag in the freezer for a while, or put an ice pack on the gum;
  2. crack off the solid pieces;
  3. sponge the remainder with eucalyptus oil or dry-cleaning fluid.
- On **carpet**:
  1. freeze with ice pack;
  2. carefully remove solid matter with blunt knife;
  3. dab with methylated spirits or white spirit.
- In **hair** (this is something that happens at least once in most families):
  1. rub some cold cream into the gummed hair;
  2. try to slide the gum off with an old dry towel or flannel;
  3. use the scissors as a last resort.

CHINA

- Wash fine china by hand in a plastic bowl or sink lined with a hand towel or rubber mat to prevent chipping. Rinse and dry.
- Clean tea and coffee stains from inside china mugs,

cups and teapots by rubbing with a damp cloth dipped in bicarbonate of soda.

- Earthenware, stoneware and salt-glaze ware are often ovenproof and can usually be washed safely in the dishwasher. Make sure that your china is dishwasher-proof before you put it in the machine.

CHOCOLATE

- On **clothing**, scrape off the solid chocolate with a blunt knife. Then, for **washable** garments, pour boiling water from a height or use detergent and work from the back of the stain, mopping as you go with a sponge. Rinse. Use laundry solvent (see SOLVENTS) to get rid of any residue. Wash as usual. Sponge **non-washable** articles with warm water and use laundry solvent.
- On **carpet**, sponge the stain with solution of 1 teaspoon of detergent, 1 teaspoon of white vinegar and 1 litre (1¾ pints) of warm water. Dry, then dab with dry-cleaning fluid or turpentine.

CHROME

- For a good polish, rub dry bicarbonate of soda on with a dry cloth.

CIGARETTE BURNS

- A cigarette burn in the **carpet** may be too deep to fix. Try lightly rubbing the burn with dry steel wool. If this fails, use a cotton bud to dab it with a weak bleach solution. Depending on the length of the carpet pile, you may be able to trim the singed sections off with small scissors (work at the pile bit by bit).

CIGARETTE SMOKE

- Clear the air of cigarette smoke by turning on exhaust fans if you can't leave windows open.
- Put small bowls of vinegar around the room where smokers are congregating.
- Burn candles during the party, and afterwards, to rid the rooms of the stale smell.
- Leave a bucket of water in the room overnight with a few slices of lemon in it.

CITRIC ACID

- A mild but useful acid which is conveniently found in a lemon.

CLOUDY AMMONIA see AMMONIA

COCKROACHES

- Sprinkle their paths liberally with highly scented talcum powder or pyrethrum powder.

COD LIVER OIL

- On **clothing**, spoon up as much of the oil as possible. Treat with dry-cleaning fluid or white vinegar on the back of the stain and then rinse.

- On **carpet**, use dry-foam carpet shampoo.
- Old stains are usually impossible to remove, but try softening them first with glycerine.

COFFEE

- Sponge stains of white coffee with warm water and borax. If the stain is old, dampen it, cover with dry borax and pour hot water through the fabric. On **carpet**, douse with soda water and blot dry with a cloth or paper towels. Sponge the residue with a solution of 1 teaspoon detergent, 1 teaspoon white vinegar and 1 litre (1¾ pints) of warm water.
- Black coffee will respond to an immediate dousing with soda water.

COFFEE MAKER

- Rinse the inside well after every brew, or traces of yesterday's coffee will cling to spoil the taste of today's fresh cup.

COMBS

- Soak in household ammonia and water and clean with a nailbrush. Rinse well and allow to dry before use.

COMPOST

- Almost half of our weekly household rubbish is food scraps, which can be recycled to contribute to the upkeep of your garden through your compost heap.

Compost bins are available from hardware shops and garden suppliers, but you can make your container without too much trouble if a heap is not suitable. If you are in an area frequented by rats and mice you'd be better off with a bin.

- Generation of heat is the key to successful compost, so the size of the heap is important; or if you use a container it must have an effective lid and sides able to keep the warmth in. Good drainage at the base is also important. If you are using a commercial bin there is no need for dampening, turning, or in any other way interfering with the compost, short of tossing a handful of lime and a handful of blood-and-bone fertilizer on top of the organic material you have added.
- You can compost most garden and vegetable matter including lawn clippings, vegetable scraps, most weeds and leaves, seaweed, spent flowers, coffee grounds, tea bags, small bits of paper and cardboard, peanut shells, the contents of vacuum cleaners, ashes and eggshells. Small meat scraps will also compost but may be better off in the dustbin to avoid attracting flies.

CONCRETE

- For an oil spill on concrete, sprinkle sand on the spill, leave it to absorb the oil, then sweep it up.
- Wet newspaper laid on a spill will absorb the oil as it dries.

COPPER

- Some modern copper products are coated, so only soap and water are needed to clean them. For uncoated copper, use Worcester sauce on a soft cloth. Polish with a dry cloth. Another method is to use salt and lemon juice mixed to a paste.

CORDUROY see VELVETEEN

CORK TILES see FLOORS

COUGH MEDICINE

- If the cough medicine is in a sugar-syrup base, wash it out with detergent and water or flush the detergent and water mixture through the fabric from the wrong side. Treat any residual stain with diluted household ammonia, then white spirit or amyl acetate.

CRAYON

- On **clothing**, apply liquid detergent and rub between your finger and thumb. For **washable** fabrics, rinse under the cold tap; for **non-washable** fabrics, sponge with cold water. Repeat if necessary. Dab with dry-cleaning fluid or white spirit. Use methylated spirits to remove any remaining stain.
- On **washable wallpaper**, use toothpaste. Rub it on gently until the crayon is removed, then wipe off. A

commercial cleaner is available for **non-washable wallpaper**.

- On **carpet**, dab with dry-cleaning fluid or turpentine. Then sponge with a solution of 1 teaspoon detergent, 1 teaspoon white vinegar and 1 litre (1¾ pints) of warm water.

CREAM

- On **clothing**, scrape up or sponge off as much as you can. Rinse in cold water. Then soak in detergent or borax solution. Dry-cleaning fluid may remove the greasy residue once the article is dry. Methylated spirits should get rid of any remaining colour.
- On **carpet**, dab with dry-cleaning fluid or turpentine. Then sponge with a solution of 1 teaspoon detergent, 1 teaspoon white vinegar and 1 litre (1¾ pints) of warm water.

CREOSOL

- Creosol is a phenol (carbolic acid) derivative found in coal tar. It is a powerful disinfectant used in lavatory cleaners and disinfectants.

CREOSOTE see CRUDE OIL

CRICKET GLOVES

- Most cricket gloves can be cleaned by scrubbing with a nailbrush and solution of 3 parts water, 2 parts methylated spirits and 1 part cloudy ammonia. Do not soak.

CRICKET TROUSERS

- The classic red stain from the cricket ball on cricket whites can be removed by sponging with warm water and wool mix (see WOOL MIX for recipe). Grass stains can be removed in the same way, then the trousers can be washed as usual. For grass stains on pure cotton trousers, see GRASS.
- Use bleach on pure cotton trousers only.

CROCHET

- Gum arabic water, made from the gum arabic powder available from artists' supply shops, is effective for stiffening fine cotton crochet table mats.

CRUDE OIL

- Soften with white spirit so that you can scrape away as much solid matter as possible. Then flush with dry-cleaning fluid. A solvent for removing crude oil is available from hardware shops.

CRYSTAL

- Don't put your crystal in the dishwasher: it is likely to crack. Wash it by hand. Add vinegar to the water, and dry by allowing to stand.
- A small chip on the rim of a crystal glass can be

repaired. Check the *Yellow Pages* for a china and crystal repairer convenient to you.

CURRY

- Soak stain with methylated spirits, diluted ammonia or white spirit.

D

DAMP CLOTHES

- Air clothes well. Don't fold them and put them away damp – you will be inviting mildew.

DAMPNESS

- To check for the source of dampness in a house, fix a piece of aluminium foil to the wall (with removable tape fixed to all 4 sides) and leave it for 24 hours. If you find moisture on the exposed surface, that's condensation. If the other side of the foil shows signs of moisture the damp is probably coming through the wall.
- To help prevent dampness in a cupboard or wardrobe, fill a tin with briquettes and punch holes in the lid. Leave the tin in the bottom of the cupboard.

DECANTERS

- Narrow-necked glass containers like decanters, carafes and vases can be cleaned by leaving them overnight filled with water containing 2 teaspoons of household ammonia. Alternatively, crush eggshells, mix with a little vinegar, place in the decanter, and shake well. Tea-leaves and vinegar also work well, and uncooked rice shaken with warm water and a dash of detergent can do the trick.
- For stubborn stains, use household bleach or dishwasher detergent mixed with water. Leave overnight.

DENIM

- Wash denim jeans before your first wear and expect them to shrink slightly unless pre-shrunk.

DENTURES

- Use one of the following methods to clean your dentures:
  - soak in white vinegar for 10–15 minutes;
  - overnight, use a solution of half vinegar and half water;
  - scrub with toothpaste and dry bicarbonate of soda. Not only will the plate be sparkling clean, but it will also taste fresh and sweet.

DETERGENTS

- Most detergents (as opposed to soaps) are based

on petroleum by-products. They contain various additives, including builders, which are mainly phosphates.

- A biological detergent includes enzymes and works better in cool than in hot water.
- Check that the products you use are biodegradable – that means that they will decompose eventually.
- Dishwashing liquid is usually a gentler detergent than laundry powders.

DIAMONDS see JEWELLERY

DISHWASHING

- An investment in a dishwasher may be an investment in happiness. But remember that the generation of electricity creates pollution and uses precious resources, so use your dishwasher sparingly. Most dishwashers have a rinse cycle, and that way you can rinse your breakfast dishes and have one big wash after dinner at night.
- For handwashing dishes (there will always be some), use the cheapest brand of dishwashing detergent but add a few tablespoons of vinegar to the washing-up water. You'll find the vinegar will cut through grease and your dishes will sparkle.
- To quickly remove food that is stuck to a casserole dish, fill with boiling water and add 2 tablespoons of baking soda or salt.

DISINFECTANT

- Disinfectant is used to kill germs and bacteria on surfaces. Chlorine bleaches, hydrogen peroxide, phenol, creosol, chloroxylenol are all used in household disinfectants.
- Both vinegar and eucalyptus oil are good disinfectants; however, eucalyptus oil is toxic and can kill useful plants and micro-organisms – so use it sparingly.

DOG

- Dry-clean your dog by sprinkling its coat liberally with bicarbonate of soda and rubbing it in. Then brush thoroughly.

DOORS

- Make your sliding doors burglar-proof by cutting a broom handle to size and placing it along the track so that the doors cannot be slid open.
- For creaking doors, see HINGES.

DRAINS

- To clean drains and clear minor blockages, flush them through with a handful of washing soda in boiling water, or a handful of bicarbonate of soda followed by 125 ml (4 fl oz) vinegar.
- If you know grease is the culprit, tip 450 g (16 oz) salt and 225 g (8 oz) baking soda down the drain and

follow it immediately with boiling water. The grease should then dissolve.

DRAWERS

- Rub the runners of the drawers with dry soap or candle wax to prevent them sticking.

DRIPPING TAPS

- Every now and then you may have to live with a dripping tap for a couple of days. If the noise is threatening your sanity, tie a piece of string or wool to the tap and direct it down the drain. The water will seep – silently – along the length of string.

DRY-CLEANING FLUID

- A dry-cleaning fluid, usually a liquid hydrocarbon, can be bought at a chemist or a hardware shop.

DUSTBINS

- Make a small hole in the lid of your plastic dustbin and tie the lid to the handle, to prevent the lid blowing away or getting lost.
- A dustbin set in an old tyre will stand upright against the fiercest wind or dog.

DUVET COVERS

- Make affordable queen-size duvet covers by sewing

together two double sheets along three sides. Use Velcro or press-studs to fasten the fourth side.

DYES

- Rinse fabric with cool water and dab with liquid detergent. If that fails to move the stain, try dabbing with methylated spirits.

E

EGG WHITES

- To keep, freeze in ice-cube trays.

EGGS

- Sponge or soak the stained fabric, using cold water. Do not apply heat or hot water, as the heat will cook the egg, making it more difficult to remove.
- Always rinse off egg in cold water. Then wash in the normal way.
- Test whether an egg is fresh by placing it in a container of water. If it sinks to the bottom, it is fresh. If it floats to the top it isn't and should be thrown away.
- Add a dash of vinegar to the pan when poaching eggs to stop them separating. Placing the eggs in boiling water for a couple of seconds before you break them also makes poaching easier.

- Before beating egg yolks, rinse the container with water and they will be easy to slide out of it.
- After hard-boiling eggs, cover them with cold water and allow them to sit until you want to use them.
- Very fresh eggs will not peel easily when hard-boiled. Use eggs at least 3 days old.

ELASTIC

- Don't use hot tumble-dryer settings for garments with elastic: it will shorten their useful life.

ELECTRIC BLANKETS

- Electric blankets should be checked for safety each year by the manufacturer. Read the safety directions, and follow the cleaning instructions to the letter: don't forget that electric blankets are potentially dangerous if not used in the manner intended.
- Don't buy an electric blanket second-hand.
- Don't put an electric blanket on a bed that a child may wet.
- Store in a plastic bag.

ELECTRIC HEATERS

- Dust the reflector on your electric heater regularly: a dusty or dull reflector reduces the heat markedly. Disconnect at the power-point before cleaning. Most reflectors can be accessed by removing a few screws and taking off the guard. Wipe over with a damp cloth.

A cloth dampened with methylated spirits will add a real shine.

- At the end of winter, store your heater in a plastic bag to keep it dust-free until the next cold spell.

EMBROIDERED ARTICLES

- Hand-wash in warm water with mild detergent, then rinse well. Iron on the wrong side to raise the pattern.

ENAMEL POTS AND PANS

- Enamel is a tough, durable surface, but it can chip if maltreated, so be sure to treat enamelware with due care and respect, according to the manufacturer's instructions.
- Use nylon pot-scourers rather than metal ones to clean the base of a burnt pan. If food is burnt on, fill it with water and a couple of teaspoons of bicarbonate of soda and bring to the boil.

ENZYMES see DETERGENTS

EPSOM SALTS

- Epsom salts (hydrated magnesium sulphate), traditionally kept in the medicine cupboard as a purgative, is now better known as a useful addition to the laundry cupboard.

ETHANOL

- Probably the most important alcohol in cleaning,

ethanol is produced by yeast during the fermentation of sugar. It dissolves grease and evaporates quickly.

EUCALYPTUS OIL

■ Oil of eucalyptus is available from the chemist and hardware shops and is handy for removing stains. It is also an essential ingredient in a wool mix (see WOOL MIX for recipe).

EYES

■ To relieve tired eyes, lie down for 10 minutes with a couple of slices of cucumber over closed eyelids.

F

FAECES

Scrape off as much as you can from the fabric and soak in a borax solution for half an hour. Then wash the article as usual.

■ See also NAPPIES.

FAT

For **cold** fat, first remove any deposit. Soak **washable** articles in biological detergent and treat remaining grease with dry-cleaning fluid. Dab **non-washable** articles with dry-cleaning fluid.

- For **hot** fat, treat **washable** and **non-washable** articles with liquid detergent and rinse or sponge with cold water. Repeat if necessary.

FAT OR OIL FIRES

- Cooking fats or oils are the cause of most kitchen fires. Watch carefully when you are frying: overheated fat or oil will begin to smoke before it bursts into flame, so remove it from the heat source at that point. The best way to control a fat or oil fire is to deny it oxygen.
- Whatever you do, *don't* put water on it or try to move the pan once the oil is on fire. Cover it with the pan lid, or smother it with salt or flour.
- A fire extinguisher or a fire blanket are both worth buying for your kitchen.

FÊTES

- Presentation plays a large part in the success of cake stalls at fêtes. Package your product beautifully and you will be surprised how much easier it is to sell. Home-made biscuits or chocolate balls packaged in small cellophane bags and tied with a ribbon will be a welcome (and relatively trouble-free) contribution.

FISH SLIME

- If possible, treat fish slime stains when wet. Soak **washable** articles in cold salted water. Then wash as usual. Send **non-washable** articles to be dry-cleaned and alert the dry-cleaner to cause of the stain.

FLEAS

- Fleas hate mint. Make sure you have some around the house.
- Fresh pine needles in the dog's kennel or underneath the dog's bed will keep dog fleas at bay. Alternatively, salt the cracks in the kennel.

FLOORS

- For **cork tiles**, mop regularly with warm soapy water to which a little methylated spirits has been added for shine. Don't wet worn cork tiles. Rub them over with mineral turpentine on a clean cloth and polish lightly.
- Never use too much water on a **timber** floor. Use a damp squeeze-mop. If it is very dirty, use a mild detergent. A timber floor can be wax-polished. A liquid wax will also help clean the floor. Oils and grease can often be removed by applying a paste of fuller's earth, soap and water. Put this on the stain and leave a day or two before removing. Do this several times if necessary.
- **Painted timber** floors need only a mild detergent.
- **Quarry tiles** may be treated with linseed oil when first laid. Leave them for at least 2 weeks before mopping them. Then damp-mop them regularly with warm water and detergent. If they eventually look dull

they can be waxed, but make sure you use a non-slip wax. A weak solution of vinegar and water will remove white marks on quarry tiles.

- **Sanded and sealed** floors should only need a light mopping with warm water. Use mild detergent if very dirty.
- Never use wax polishes, turpentine or paraffin on **rubber** floors.
- Don't wash **slate** floors with detergent or soap as it will leave a film. Wash with warm water and washing soda if necessary and apply lemon juice to give a brilliant shine.
- For **terrazzo** floors see TERRAZZO.
- For **varnished** floors, a damp mop with a little detergent added is all that's necessary.
- Use warm sudsy water for **vinyl** floors. Some of the liquid laundry detergents are excellent for vinyl floors. Add a tablespoon of fabric softener to give a brilliant shine.

FLOUR COATING

- Put the flour and seasoning in a plastic bag, add the meat or fish, shake well, and leave in the bag for a while if desired.

FLOWERS

- The following hints will help you get the best results from your cut flowers:

- Flowers in a vase don't appreciate being crowded: fewer flowers per vase will last longer.
- Always cut stems at an angle, with very sharp scissors or knife. Recut the stems every couple of days.
- Split the ends of thick stems before arranging the flowers. This gives them a better chance to absorb moisture. For poppies, hellebores and hydrangeas, burn the cut ends over a candle to prevent the blooms from wilting.
- Remove leaves below the waterline, or rotting leaves will foul the water and give off an unpleasant smell.
- Two tablespoons of vinegar and 2 tablespoons of sugar per litre (1¾ pints) of water will prolong the life of most flowers. The vinegar inhibits the growth of organisms and the sugar serves as food.
- Add a teaspoon of sugar to a vase of marigolds. It will prevent an unpleasant smell developing.
- Carnations will last longer if placed in water containing a little boric acid.
- To keep water from clouding in a clear vase, add 1 tablespoon of liquid bleach to 1 litre (1¾ pints) of water.

FLOWER COLOURING

- Change the colour of your cut flowers by putting food dye in warm water and standing the stems in the solution overnight. By morning you will see the coloured water has been absorbed into the flowers.

FLOWER STAINS see GRASS

FLY SPOTS

- Cold tea will remove fly spots from mirrors.

FOOD-COLOURING DYE

- Try flushing out with cold water first. Turn the tap briefly on full and the force of the water will flush out much of the dye without spreading the stain. Then rub powdered detergent into the stain between your finger and thumb and rinse again in cold water. Finally soak in cool detergent suds for 30 minutes, and then wash as usual.

FROSTING GLASS

- If you need to frost a pane of glass temporarily, mix together 2 tablespoons of Epsom salts with 125 ml (4 fl oz) stale beer or brown vinegar. Dab mixture over the clean window. Put on another coat if necessary.

FRUIT

- Rinse or sponge at once in cold water (before the stain dries).
- Remove older stains from **washable** clothing or household linen by stretching the stained area over a

bowl and pouring boiling water through the stain. Alternatively, use a biological soaker or spray, then wash as usual.

- Most fruit will ripen easily if put in a brown-paper bag with an apple.

FULLER'S EARTH

- A clay mineral in the form of an absorbent powder, fuller's earth is good for removing grease from **non-washable** upholstery and fabrics.

FURNITURE POLISH

- Make your own furniture polish. Mix together 85 ml (3 fl oz) each of boiled linseed oil, turpentine and vinegar and shake well. Apply it with a soft cloth and wipe completely dry. Then wipe again with another soft cloth. *Don't* try to boil your own linseed oil: it is available from a hardware shop.
- Alternatively, mix 2 parts of olive oil to 1 part of lemon juice and shake well. Apply with a soft cloth.
- To remove furniture polish stain from a **carpet**, dab with dry-cleaning fluid, lighter fuel or turpentine. Then sponge with a solution of 1 teaspoon of detergent, 1 teaspoon of white vinegar and 1 litre (1¾ pints) of water.

G

GARAGE FLOORS

- To remove oil from a floor, sprinkle the spill with sand or cat litter. This will absorb the oil and you can then sweep it up.

GARLIC

- Garlic cloves can be kept fresh in a jar filled to the brim with cooking oil. The oil can then be used to add some extra flavour to salad dressing.

GARLIC GARDEN SPRAY

- Crush 85 g garlic cloves and soak in 2 tablespoons neat paraffin for 48 hours. Use 7 g soap flakes and 600 ml (18 fl oz) water to make a soap mixture, add to the garlic clove mixture and strain. Store in a jar or bottle, labelled and out of reach of children. Add 1 part mixture to 50 parts water when spraying.

GENTIAN VIOLET

- For a gentian violet stain on **fabric**, use calamine lotion or rub gently with methylated spirits.
- On **carpet**, massage in a paste of methylated spirits and borax. Leave the stain covered and let it dry, then

vacuum off. Keep repeating, rubbing the paste further into the carpet fibres, as the stain fades.

GILT FRAMES

- Remove discolouration from a gilt frame by wiping with equal parts of water and methylated spirits or rubbing with a piece of lemon and sponging with 1 teaspoon of baking soda to half a litre (¾ pint) of warm water. Use a chamois to buff it.

GLASS

- Wearing rubber gloves, wipe up broken glass with something you can dispose of along with the glass – damp cottonwool, tissues, or an old cloth.

GLASS STOPPERS

- If a glass stopper gets stuck in a container, pour a little warm cooking oil around the neck and the stopper and try again in a few minutes.

GLASS TABLETOPS

- Wipe a glass tabletop with a ball of crumpled newspaper dampened with either white vinegar or methylated spirits. Polish with dry newspaper for a sparkle.

GLASSWARE

- Delicate glass will crack from sudden expansion if put in hot water bottom first. Slip it in sideways and it will survive.

- Line the sink with an old towel or cloth when washing valuable and delicate glassware.
- Add a dash of ammonia to the rinsing water for an added sparkle.
- See also CRYSTAL

GLUE see ADHESIVES

GOLDEN SYRUP

- To measure spoonfuls of golden syrup or honey accurately, heat the spoon in hot water first and the syrup will run off cleanly. Alternatively, heat the honey or syrup briefly.
- If honey has crystallized in the bottom of the jar, stand it in hot water until it softens.

GRASS

- Attack grass stains as soon as possible. If the material is **cotton**, soak in a mixture of 2 parts methylated spirits to 1 part cloudy ammonia and 3 parts hot water. Rinse before washing.
- For stains on **synthetics**, work wool mix (see WOOL MIX for recipe) into the stain and then wash as usual.
- On **knitted** fabrics, cover the dampened stain with toothpaste, leave for half an hour, then rinse away with warm water.
- On **carpet**, use methylated spirits.

GRATERS

- To make the clean-up easier, rub with salad oil before using.
- An old toothbrush will get rid of lemon rind, cheese or onion before the grater is washed.

GRAVY

- On **fabric**, wipe off excess gravy then flush or soak in cold water. Use dry-cleaning fluid on any stain that is still there.
- On **carpet**, use carpet shampoo.

GREASE AND OIL

- Treat immediately. On **fabric**, use absorbent paper and iron with a warm iron, changing the paper frequently; or sponge with white spirit or dry-cleaning fluid. Then rinse, and wash in warm soapy water. **Non-washable** articles should be treated with a warm iron on absorbent paper or by dusting with absorbent powder. Let dry, then brush off. Repeat if necessary. Dry-cleaning fluid may also work.
- On **carpet**, dab with dry-cleaning fluid, lighter fuel or turpentine. Work inwards from the edge of the stain.
- On **concrete**, use 1 part detergent to 6 parts paraffin. Leave for a few minutes, then hose with clean water.

GROUT

- Clean discoloured grout with a toothbrush and a

bathroom cleaner, or with a solution of household bleach and water.

GUMBOOTS

- Buy your children gumboots a size larger than necessary and they can initially wear 2 pairs of socks. That way you can get 2 seasons out of 1 pair.

H

HAIR

- Remove animal hair from carpet and furniture by wiping over with a sponge dampened with white vinegar and water.

HAIR DYE

- Rinse fabric immediately with cold water, then wash in warm water with liquid detergent. Add a little cloudy ammonia to final rinse. Treat residual stains with white spirit and if staining persists, with hydrogen peroxide solution. Rinse well.

HAIRBRUSH

- Clean your hairbrush in shampoo and warm water, and dry it with the hair-dryer if you are in a hurry.

HAIRSPRAY

- Remove hairspray from mirrors with methylated spirits.

HANDBAGS

- To retain a handbag's shape when it is not in use, pack it with the paper it was sold with – or use newspaper.

HANGING PICTURES

- Never use natural fibres (for example, string or cotton) to hang a picture, as the fibre may rot, causing your picture to fall off the wall. Use nylon cord or fuse wire.

HATS

- Perspiration stains on the inside edge of a hat can be removed by using a toothbrush – with eucalyptus oil, or soap with a few drops of cloudy ammonia.

HEAT MARKS ON POLISHED FURNITURE

- Rub *lightly* with methylated spirits on a soft cloth. Apply an oily polish and leave it on the stain for 24 hours. Then rub the polish off with a soft cloth. Alternatively, rub *gently* with fine steel wool before applying polish.

HEMLINES

- Letting down a school winter tunic? Sponge the old

hemline mark with diluted vinegar on a damp cloth, then bunch it and rinse it under a cold tap. Use a towel to press out as much water as you can, then cover the wet area with a dry cloth and press with a hot iron.

HINGES

■ If your door starts to creak, inspect the hinges. Remove dirt with a toothbrush and use Vaseline or sewing-machine oil on the mechanism. Wipe off excess. Alternatively, rub with a cake of soap.

HONEY see GOLDEN SYRUP

HORN see IVORY HANDLES

HOT-WATER BOTTLES

If a rubber hot-water bottle is in need of cleaning, soak in a mild detergent in hot water for up to 5 minutes. A toothbrush, nailbrush or sponge can be used on the ridges if necessary.

HOUSE PLANTS

■ To keep your indoor plants heading for the ceiling rather than the window, turn the pots regularly so that they absorb the available sunlight evenly. This will encourage them to grow straight.

■ Dust plant leaves with a feather duster. If you wish to

give them an extra gloss, use a few drops of glycerine on a cloth.

- To water your house plants quickly, efficiently and without mess, put 2 or 3 ice-cubes in each pot.
- If you are going away for a couple of weeks, put your house plants in the bath on an old towel, and run in 5–10 cm (2–4 in) cold water. There will be a tropical jungle when you get back.

HYDRANGEAS

- To preserve hydrangeas, stand the stems in 1 part glycerine to 2 parts water and leave for 5 days, topping up each day with water as the liquid is absorbed.

HYDROGEN PEROXIDE

- Hydrogen peroxide, responsible for many a teenage blonde, is a disinfectant and bleach available at chemists. It usually comes in 20-volume strength and for most jobs is diluted 1 part hydrogen peroxide to 6 parts water.
- Don't leave coloured fabrics in hydrogen peroxide solution for more than 20 minutes.

I

ICE

■ Build up a supply of ice-cubes for drinks by transferring batches from trays to plastic bags in your freezer.

ICE-CREAM

✱ For ice-cream on **fabric**, scrape off any solid matter with a blunt knife. Soak in warm water and detergent. Any remaining stain can be treated with dry-cleaning fluid.

■ On **carpet**, sponge with a mixture of 1 teaspoon of detergent, 1 teaspoon of white vinegar and a litre (1¾ pints) of warm water.

ICE-CREAM CONTAINERS

■ While plastic ice-cream containers are ideal for storage, don't use them to heat up food in the microwave. Most are unsafe for microwave use.

INDELIBLE PENCIL

✱ Don't wet the stain or it will spread. Use dry-cleaning fluid until no more dye appears on the cloth. When dry, rub liquid detergent lightly into the stain and wash in the usual way.

INK

- **Indelible** or **printer's** ink must be caught at once *before it dries*, or it may be with you for ever, just as the manufacturer promises. If you don't catch it in time, try dabbing with 1 dessertspoon of oxalic acid in 250 ml (8 fl oz) warm water. Then rinse in water to which some bicarbonate of soda has been added. Oxalic acid, available from chemists, *must be used with great care*. Protect your hands, arms and face, and wash off any spills at once. Keep out of reach of children.
- Hairspray will remove **ballpoint pen** from vinyl furniture.
- Some **felt-tipped pens** are designed to be permanent. When buying felt-tipped pens for children, be sure to buy the **non-indelible** ones, which will wash out reasonably easily if they mark clothing or furniture.

INSECTS

- Citronella, available from chemists and health stores, is a good insect repellent.
- See also ANTS; BLUEBOTTLES; MOSQUITOES; MOTHS; SILVERFISH; WASPS.

INSTRUCTION LEAFLETS

- File all the instruction leaflets for electrical appliances and children's toys together. Read the leaflets – you'll be amazed at how much time you save by reading the instructions first.

IODINE

- Dampen the stain and place somewhere warm: in the sun, on a radiator or even in the steam from the kettle. Then place in boiling water if the material permits; otherwise, wash in the usual way.

IRON

- To clean the outside of your iron, use toothpaste as the iron cools.

IRONING

- Folding the washing as you take it off the clothes-line makes ironing much easier.
- Make ironing more pleasant by keeping within range of the radio, television or record-player.
- Iron only what *needs* to be ironed. A good rule is: if it doesn't show, don't iron it.
- Use paper clips to hold pleats in place as you iron.
- Iron embroidery right side down on a soft towel – to raise the pattern.
- Turn the iron off at the switch if you are interrupted while you are ironing.
- Always empty a steam iron immediately after use.

IVORY HANDLES

■ Never put cutlery with ivory or bone handles in the dishwasher; they will discolour and spoil. Don't wash the handles in hot water as this will cause them to discolour faster. Wash them quickly in warm water, and dry them thoroughly.

J

JAM

✾ Remove jam stains from **washable** fabric by soaking in a solution of borax and water; then wash as usual. In the case of **non-washable** garments, tell the dry-cleaner what the stain is.

JARS

■ To clean musty or smelly jars, half fill with cold water and add one tablespoon of dry mustard. Shake and stand for 20 minutes, then rinse thoroughly.

JEWELLERY

■ If a fine chain is knotted, lay the knot in a drop of salad oil and undo it with the help of 2 pins.
■ Keep jewellery clean and store it carefully in separate boxes or in a jewellery roll.

- Wash jewellery in warm water. Don't use hot water because it may loosen the settings. Rinse in warm water and dry gently in a soft cloth. Household ammonia may help loosen the more stubborn dirt – but whatever you do, *don't* use it on **pearls** or **coral**.
- For **diamonds**, add some soap flakes and a few drops of ammonia to warm water. Soak your jewellery in the solution. Rinse, dry, dip into a little white spirit, and allow to dry again.
- Soak **emeralds** in mild tepid suds and clean the setting gently with your fingers or a soft make-up brush. Rinse, and dry with a soft cloth.
- Soak **gold** in a little cloudy ammonia for up to 10 minutes. Rinse, and dry with a soft cloth. Use an old toothbrush to clean the tricky bits.
- Wipe your **opals** clean with a soft cloth.
- Rub **pearls** gently with a clean soft chamois.
- Use a clean chamois to clean **platinum**.
- For **rubies**, mix together 250 ml (8 fl oz) warm water, 70 ml (2 fl oz) of ammonia and a tablespoon of dishwashing detergent. Soak the piece in the liquid for 10 minutes. Then, if necessary, scrub gently with an old toothbrush. Rinse in warm water and dunk in methylated spirits. Pat dry with a cloth or a tissue.
- Clean **silver** with a silver polish specially formulated for jewellery. Alternatively, line the bottom of a saucepan with a piece of aluminium foil and warm 500 ml (16 fl oz) water and 1 dessertspoon of either washing

soda or bicarbonate of soda. Place the jewellery in a wire strainer and immerse it thoroughly. Rinse, and dry on a soft towel.

JUMPERS

- Use old tights or stockings to hang up the woollen jumpers you like to line-dry.

K

KAPOK

- Kapok is made from the seed pods of the kapok tree and is one of the materials used for stuffing cushions or pillows. Dry-clean only: this stuffing doesn't wash well.

KETTLES

- To remove fur and scale from an electric kettle, cover the element with equal parts of vinegar and water, bring to the boil and allow to cool, then pour out. Then boil up some water and tip that out before using the kettle again.

KEYS

- Tape a spare ignition key somewhere out of sight on

your car to relieve those awful moments when you realize you've locked your keys in the car.

- To make your keys easier to find in your handbag, put a bright-coloured tab on your key ring.

KNITTED GARMENTS

- Knitted woollen garments (even **machine-washable** ones) should be washed gently. Never wring out a knitted garment.
- To remove excess water from a **non-machine-washable** woollen garment after hand-washing, squeeze gently, then remove most moisture by spreading it on a bath towel and rolling it and the towel up together.
- Alternatively, hand-wash the garment, fold in a towel and spin *for a few seconds* in the washing machine.

KNITTING

- Keep a crochet hook with your knitting to pick up those inevitable dropped stitches.

KNIVES

- **Stainless steel** kitchen knives should be the choice for everyday use, and a good one is an investment you will never regret. Buy one that has the blade integrated with the handle. The knife should be kept sharp with a steel (always warm a knife before sharpening it), and should be professionally sharpened from time to time as well.

- Store kitchen knives in a wooden block or a lined drawer. Keeping sharp knives loose in ordinary drawers is bad for the knives, which will be blunted or chipped, and dangerous for anyone who is searching for cutlery.
- You may own a **carbon steel** knife you use for special jobs. Rust will appear on the surface if you put it in the dishwasher, or leave it wet. Wash at once by hand, and dry thoroughly. Don't use a rusted or discoloured knife. To remove a build-up of rust, rub gently with the finest sandpaper ('wet-and-dry'). For carbon steel knives you use rarely, coat the blades with Vaseline and wrap in greaseproof paper to store.

L

LABELS

- To remove labels from **bottles** or **jars**, soak in hot water until softened.
- Stubborn stick-on labels, and the adhesive left behind when they are removed, will often respond to rubbing with methylated spirits. If that doesn't work, acetone or non-oily nail-polish remover will.

- Printed labels stuck on **fabric** can be removed by sponging the label with methylated spirits and ironing the reverse of the garment with a hot iron.

LACE

- Lace can be made of cotton, nylon, polyester, or a mixture.
- Hand-wash in warm soapy water, using soap flakes. **Delicate** lace should be washed as rarely as possible. Pin it in place on a linen-covered board and sponge soiled areas gently with soapy water. **More robust** lace trimmings can be machine-washed on the most gentle cycle, or the lace can be put in a cloth bag and dunked up and down in mild suds.
- Always cover with a cloth before ironing.

LACQUER

- Treat a lacquer stain with amyl acetate for as long as it takes to remove the stain. Alternatively, try flushing the stain with dry-cleaning fluid.

LACQUERED FURNITURE

- Wipe with a damp chamois and polish with a soft duster.

LAMBSWOOL see SHEEPSKINS

LAMINATED SURFACES

- To remove difficult marks, wipe with methylated

spirits; then rinse well. Alternatively, use bicarbonate of soda on a damp cloth.

LAMPSHADES

- Dust regularly using a cloth, feather duster or the dusting brush on the vacuum cleaner.
- A **washable** lampshade can be washed in the bath if it is too big for the laundry trough. But take care: the fabric may be washable, but is the glue that holds it together? Most fabric lampshades can be dry-cleaned.
- Clean **paper** lampshades by dusting with powdered starch, cornflour or talcum powder. Leave for 24 hours, then dust.
- **Plastic** and **glass** shades can be wiped over with a cloth wrung out in warm water and dishwashing detergent.

LANOLIN

- Lanolin is a fatty substance extracted from sheep's wool. It can be used to soften rough skin and to condition leather.

LAUNDRY SOLVENT see SOLVENTS

LAVATORIES see TOILETS

LEATHER see also SHOES

- Never store leather garments under plastic, as leather needs to breathe.

LEATHER GLOVES

- Wash leather gloves in warm soapy water while you are wearing them. Dry over a bottle, away from direct heat. When they are dry, put them on and gently rub your hands together to soften the leather.

LEATHER LUGGAGE

- Use saddle soap for cleaning leather luggage. Lanolin or castor oil will help you keep the leather supple.

LEATHER UPHOLSTERY

- Vacuum the leather gently, then wipe down with a soft cloth, cleaning the backs of chairs and couches and down beside the arms. Every 6 months or so, wash the leather using lukewarm water and laundry soap. Dry the leather and then dress it with the hide food recommended by the manufacturer.

LEAVES

- Dampen your autumn leaves before you attempt to sweep them up. Then put them in the compost or on the garden beds; don't burn them.

LEMONS

- Keep lemons for cleaning and bleaching as well as for cooking.
- Warm lemons yield more juice. Fifteen minutes in hot water (or 15 seconds in a microwave) will do the trick.

- If the recipe calls for lemon juice but no rind, squeeze the juice and put the rind in the freezer. When you need it, the rind can be grated without thawing.
- When lemons are plentiful, squeeze them and freeze the juice in an ice-cube tray. Once frozen they can be stored in a freezer bag. Alternatively, store lemons for juice by freezing the fruit whole.
- Always leave a short stem when storing lemons out of the freezer. Don't store with oranges: both may go mouldy.

LETTUCE see SALAD GREENS

LICHEN

- Remove slippery lichen from paving by dousing it with a bucket of hot water containing 12 tablespoons (225 g/8 oz) washing soda.

LIDS

- To loosen lids, use a damp kitchen sponge or cloth, or a rubber glove, to increase your grip. Up-end stubborn screw-on lids in hot water and then try again. Sandpaper held firmly around a lid may also do the trick.

LINEN

- Linen is woven from yarns made from flax fibres. Follow the manufacturer's cleaning instructions: not all linens should be washed.

LINOLEUM

- 'Lino', as it is called, is a natural material based on finely ground cork and linseed oil. Genuine lino is almost a thing of the past: the more robust vinyl flooring has usurped its role.
- Mop linoleum with warm water and detergent. Steel wool dipped in turpentine will remove marks – but be careful that you don't remove the gloss as well.

LINSEED OIL

- Linseed oil, made from common flax seeds, has very little smell. Two types are available: raw linseed oil and boiled linseed oil. Do not attempt to boil your own oil: the result will not be the same and the oil is highly flammable.

LINT

- Use clear adhesive tape or masking tape to collect the lint off clothing. Alternatively, try a damp flannel – dark coloured for dark clothing.

LIPSTICK

- For lipstick on **fabric**, try cold water first and, if that fails, put glycerine on the stain, leave overnight, then wash in warm to hot sudsy water. On **carpet**, try eucalyptus oil.
- Mend a broken lipstick by warming the fractured ends

over a candle flame and pushing them together. Coo in the fridge.

LOOFAHS

- To remove the soap build-up and the slimy feel, soal a loofah or sponge in water with a tablespoon o vinegar added.

LOOSE COVERS

- Some loose covers for furniture are machine washable but too bulky for a domestic machine. Wash these at the laundromat. Other covers may be dry-cleanable only: inquire about cleaning requirements when you buy.

LYE

- Lye is a general term for the strong alkalis used for various cleaning operations and in various cleaning preparations, for example, drain clearers and many lavatory cleaners. The most common lye for domestic use is sodium hydroxide or caustic soda, which must be used with caution and as a last resort.
- See also CAUSTIC SODA.

M

MARBLE

- The type of care needed will depend on the surface of the marble. You should dust **polished** marble or wipe it clean with a soft damp cloth.
- Clean stains on **unpolished** marble with lemon juice or vinegar, being careful not to leave it more than a minute before you rinse and dry. Try undiluted liquid detergent to remove light stains. If that fails, try toothpaste. A polish with a soft cloth moistened with turpentine will bring the sheen back. Beeswax furniture polish also gives a good finish.
- Wipe **worktops** with a cloth dipped in water to which liquid detergent has been added. Be careful not to let moisture soak into the marble. Wipe over with half a lemon, or vinegar.

MARINADE

- A marinade, made with various ingredients, usually acts as a tenderizer and can enhance the flavour of a cut of meat. The meat is usually soaked in the marinade for at least 3 hours.
- A marinade particularly suitable for **steak** is made up as follows.

185 ml (6½ fl oz) red wine
60 ml (2 fl oz) olive oil
1 onion, chopped
1 clove garlic, crushed
1 bay leaf
peppercorns
parsley

Soak meat in the marinade for 3 hours at least, turning it several times. Spoon marinade over the meat as it is cooking.

MASCARA

- When mascara appears to be finished or dry, immerse the container in a cup of hot water for a few minutes. You'll find you have enough for one last application.

MASKING TAPE

- Use masking tape to save clean-up time when painting mirrors or windows.
- Keep a roll of masking tape handy in the kitchen to reseal packets of food.
- See also LINT.

MAYONNAISE

- For mayonnaise stains on **fabric**, first sponge off as much as you can. Rinse in cold water, then wash in biological detergent or a solution of 2 tablespoons borax to 500 ml (¾ pint) water. If a stain remains when fabric is dry, try spot-cleaning with dry-cleaning fluid; then rinse, and wash as usual. On **carpet**, treat with dry-cleaning fluid.

- When making mayonnaise, ensure the eggs you use are at room temperature. Taken straight from the fridge they will curdle.

MEASURING-JUG

- A handy measuring-jug is the glassware type that is both microwave-proof, so that it can be used for heating liquids, and dishwasher-proof.

MEAT JUICES

- For a meat-juice stain on **fabric**, act as soon as possible. Rinse under a cold tap, then in some liquid detergent. Rinse and allow to dry. Treat any remaining stain with dry-cleaning fluid.
- On **carpet**, dab with dry-cleaning fluid, rubbing inwards so that the stain will not be spread.

MEAT MINCER

- To make cleaning easier and to collect the last of the meat, put a piece of bread through the mincer before dismantling it.

METAL FURNITURE

- Rust can be removed from metal furniture by rubbing with mineral turpentine.

METAL POLISH

- For a stain on fabric, flush with water, then work in some liquid detergent and rinse.

METHYLATED SPIRITS

- Methylated spirits is ethanol with additives. It is useful for a number of tasks, but particularly for cleaning mirrors, glass, ceramic tiles and laminated surfaces.

METRIC CONVERSIONS

- See the tables at the back of this book.

MICROWAVE OVEN

- Wipe with a damp cloth after each use.
- Remove cooking odours by boiling some lemon juice and water in the oven for about 5 minutes.

MILDEW

- Paraffin will remove some mildew stains, particularly on **washable** fabrics. Soak the mildew spots in paraffin, leave overnight and wash in warm sudsy water.
- Household bleach is effective on suitable fabrics. Follow the directions on the bottle.

MILK

- For a milk stain on **fabric**, rinse in cold water, then soak in detergent and lukewarm water with a drop or two of household ammonia added. Rinse, and wash in lukewarm water.

- On **upholstery**, sponge with cold water and dab with dry-cleaning fluid.
- On **carpet**, sponge with lukewarm water. Dab with dry-cleaning fluid, then sponge again, using warm water with a dash of white vinegar and detergent.

MINERAL OIL

- Treat the stain first with dry-cleaning fluid, then rinse. Rub on some lemon juice and rinse again.

MINERAL TURPENTINE

- Mineral turpentine is a volatile oil derived from coniferous trees. It is used in mixing paints, varnishes and in medicines, and is useful as a household cleaner, particularly for removing stubborn marks and grease from timber.

MIRRORS

- Clean with a soft cloth or a squeegee and finish off with a chamois. Cold tea will remove flyspecks. Methylated spirits will remove hairspray from a mirror.

MOHAIR

- Wash mohair garments in shampoo to make the most of their softness.

MOSQUITOES

- A few drops of spirits of camphor on a lump of sugar placed on your bedside table will keep mosquitoes away.

MOTHER-OF-PEARL

- Use soap and water for cleaning mother-of-pearl. Don't use ammonia.

MOTHS

- Moth larvae can ruin clothes and carpets. Pest strips or mothballs are effective, but remember that *both* must be kept out of reach of children.
- If you use mothballs, hang stored clothes on the clothes-line to get rid of the mothball smell. Whole cloves or sprigs of wormwood added to your jumper storage in summer will also help, and they have a more pleasant smell than mothballs. Epsom salts sprinkled at the back of drawers and cupboards will also act as a deterrent.

MOULD see MILDEW

MUD

- Don't try to treat a mud stain on a carpet while it is still wet, other than removing the solid matter. Allow it to dry and then sweep or vacuum up as much as possible. The remainder can be treated with dry-cleaning fluid.

- Alternatively, pour salt on the wet mud, leave to dry, then vacuum.

MUESLI

- Make your own muesli with rolled oats, mixed dried fruits (apricots, sultanas, apples, pears, peaches), oat bran, wheat germ, sesame seeds, lecithin meal or granules, sunflower seeds and anything else that takes your fancy. Rolled oats is usually the main ingredient, but proportions can be varied to suit your taste.

MULBERRY

- Mulberry stains on your hands will disappear miraculously if you rub them with green mulberries and wash with warm water.

MUSTARD

- A mustard stain is almost impossible to remove once dry, so act quickly. On **fabric**, rinse under a cold tap. Treat with liquid detergent, then rinse again. On **upholstery**, sponge with cold water, then use ammonia or dry-cleaning fluid.

N

NAIL POLISH

- To quick-dry your nail polish, put your fingertips in a bowl of ice-water and leave for 2 minutes.
- To ensure that you'll always be able to open the nail-polish bottle, rub some Vaseline inside the lid and around the neck.
- Store your nail polish in the fridge and it will go on easily and smoothly. Alternatively, keep some nail-polish thinner on your shelf and add a drop as you need it.
- For nail polish on **clothing**, use a non-oily nail-polish remover or acetone as long as the garment you are treating is not an acetate fabric. If it is, use amyl acetate. Remove traces of colour with methylated spirits.
- On **carpet**, remove a dry spill with nail-polish remover.
- Allow a spill on a **floor** to dry before you attempt to remove it. Once dry, you should be able to peel if off in one piece.

NAIL-POLISH REMOVER

- Nail-polish remover is highly flammable. Do not

smoke when you are using it and keep it well away from any naked flame.

- See also ACETONE.

NAILS

- When hammering nails, secure them by first hammering them through a piece of cardboard or placing them between the teeth of an old comb – and save your fingers.

NAPPIES

- Various commercial nappy cleaners simply require you to soak the rinsed soiled nappy for 24 hours and then rinse again.
- To rinse a soiled nappy, hang on securely to one end and flush the faeces into the toilet.

NAPPY PINS

- Run a nappy pin through your hair before using it to secure your child's nappy. The natural oils from your hair are enough to ensure the pin will glide easily through the material.

NEEDLES

- When threading a needle, thread the end you've just cut off the cotton reel. The cotton is then less likely to knot.
- Thread several needles before you begin a hand-sewing task. Then you'll be able to work more continuously.

- When gathering a large piece of fabric by hand, threa the needle but don't cut the cotton off the reel. Tha way you'll never have the infuriating experience o running out of cotton half-way through the gatherin operation.
- Store your loose needles in a cork. Alternatively, stor them with the threads still in place: they'll be ready fo a quick mending job, and easy to see.

NET CURTAINS

- Net curtains should be washed regularly, as once the are really dirty they are almost impossible to ge clean. Wash *very* gently.

NEWSPAPERS

- Newspapers can be used on your garden beds. Simpl rip into strips and immerse in water until sodden then dig into your garden. Strips of newspaper ca also be added to your compost. Use sheets of news paper as mulch around plants.
- Newspapers can also be used as fuel for your fire. Soa for a few days in water then roll into tight balls or log and allow to dry.

NICKEL

- Rub nickel surfaces with a cloth moistened wit methylated spirits.

NICOTINE

- Nicotine stains on fingers can be removed with a mixture of sugar and lemon juice.

NON-STICK POTS AND PANS see TEFLON

NUTS

- If nuts are hard to crack, place them in a warm oven for 15 minutes and try again.

NYLON FABRICS

- Nylon in its 'natural' state is grey, so be careful not to wash the white pigment out by using very hot water. Hot water also tends to set the creases in nylon.
- Don't use blue detergents for pale nylon, or wash with dark colours.
- Soak discoloured nylon in warm water with 2 tablespoons of methylated spirits and 1 teaspoon of ammonia. After 10 minutes, wash in warm suds and rinse.

O

OATS see MUESLI

ODOURS

- Here's how to deal with some unpleasant household smells:
  - Don't leave **cigarette butts** in an ashtray overnight. Empty the ashtrays into an airtight container or into the dustbin outside. A few slices of lemon in a bucket of water will rid the room of the stale smell.
  - Vinegar will help get rid of the smell of **fish** from plates and glassware. Add a teaspoon to the washing-up water. Dry mustard will also work on most kitchen utensils. Sprinkle it on, leave it for a while, then wash as usual. Or you can add a teaspoon of mustard to the washing-up water for a similar effect.
  - To remove the smell of **fresh paint**, place 2 large chopped onions in a bucket of water in the middle of the room.
  - To deal with smells in a **microwave** oven, add 125 ml (4 fl oz) lemon juice to 250 ml (8 fl oz) water and boil the mixture in the oven for a few minutes.

– A small open box of bicarbonate of soda will keep your **fridge** odour-free. Replace it every couple of months.
– A solution of bicarbonate of soda and water sponged on to the affected area should remove the odour of **vomit**.

OIL see GREASE

OIL FIRES see FAT OR OIL FIRES

OIL PAINT see PAINTING

OINTMENT STAINS

❧ Try dry-cleaning solution, then rinse in cold water. Then work in liquid detergent and rinse again.

OLIVE OIL

■ Olive oil is a mono-unsaturated oil which is nutritious as well as an essential ingredient for many dishes. Virgin olive oils are taken from the first pressing of the olives and are more expensive than most refined olive oils, which are made from the pulp of the first pressing.

ONION

■ Take the tears out of slicing onions by:
– peeling and slicing under cold water;

– chopping the root end of the onion last;
– freezing or refrigerating the onion before chopping

ONION ODOUR

■ To get rid of the smell of onion from your hands, rub them with baking powder, then rinse.

ORANGES

■ When oranges are sweet and in season, freeze the juice in ice-cube trays, then place in plastic bags. I will keep for up to 6 months.

■ Oranges cut into quarters and frozen make good ice blocks for children.

■ To make peeling easier, put oranges in hot water for a few minutes and the pith will come away with the skin.

OREGANO

■ Oregano is a strong and aromatic herb. It enhance egg and cheese dishes as well as pork, lamb, poultry pasta sauces and pizza toppings.

ORGANDIE

■ Organdie is a fine crisp cotton or nylon fabric. **Nylon** organdie should be washed as nylon. Hand-wash **cotton** organdie according to washing instructions on the garment, or find out the washing procedure when buying the fabric.

ORGANZA

- Organza is stiffened chiffon, and may be made of silk or various other fibres. Hand-wash according to washing instructions on the garment, or find out the washing procedure when buying the fabric.

ORIENTAL RUGS

- Valuable oriental rugs need expert care. Refer to the place of purchase, or look up Carpet Cleaning in the *Yellow Pages*.

OUTDOOR COOKING

- The microwave can be used to partially cook food you intend to barbecue, speeding up the meal and putting an end to half-raw chicken and pork.

OVEN

- Wipe the inside of your oven while it is still hot after each use. If you are aware of a spill during cooking, sprinkle salt on it. When it has cooled you will be able to brush it off and clean the remainder with a damp cloth.
- 250 ml (8 fl oz) water mixed with 125 ml (4 fl oz) cloudy ammonia left to stand in a warm oven for at least 15 minutes should enable you to wipe away most of the grease with a sponge and warm sudsy water. You can resort to *gentle* scouring and bicarbonate of soda for the really hard-to-move grease.

OVEN BAGS

■ You will be amazed at the speed with which an oven bag cooks the Christmas turkey. It can more than halve the cooking time. Save energy, and oven-cleaning, by using oven bags for all meat and poultry roasting.

OVENPROOF DISHES

■ Some ovenproof dishes can be used on your cooking top, but not all – so check before you put your best ovenproof casserole on the stove top to bring its contents to the boil. Transfer the contents to a pan rather than risk a disaster.

OVERALLS

- Dirty overalls should be washed separately. Before washing, dampen them and rub a laundry soap into the stains, leaving them rolled up tightly overnight before machine-washing. Keep the water level on the machine on HIGH, even if they are the only item in it.
- Greasy overalls may benefit from a thorough sprinkling with inexpensive talcum powder. Rub it in, roll up and leave it overnight; then shake it free the next morning. The powder should take some of the grease with it.

OYSTERS

■ Oysters can be steamed in their shells in a microwave on MEDIUM for 3–4 minutes per dozen. Those that don't open are bad and should be thrown away.

P

PAINT

- Paint stains are best caught while still wet. It is worth inquiring at the place of purchase about a proprietary paint remover if you have a real problem.
- For an **acrylic** paint stain, absorb as much as possible first, then use detergent solution on the remainder. Dry-cleaning fluid or white spirit can be used on any residue.
- Treat **enamel** paint with paint remover or white spirit while wet.
- Sponge wet **oil** paint with dry-cleaning fluid or white spirit, then rinse.
- Once a paint stain on **carpet** has dried you will have to live with it, so work out nifty ways of rearranging your furniture to cover it.

PAINTBRUSHES

- Soften hard paintbrushes by soaking them in hot vinegar for at least an hour, then washing them in warm soapy water.
- If you are interrupted while painting or want to take a short break, wrap your paintbrush in plastic cling film and it will not harden.

PAINTING

- Use old newspapers to work the paint out of your brush when you finish for the day.
- Dig your nails into a bar of soap before you start painting (this works well for gardening too) to keep them clean.
- When painting a chair or table, put jam-jar or ice-cream-container lids under each of the legs to catch the drips.
- When painting around windows, use masking tape to keep the glass paint-free. If wide areas need to be masked for spray-painting, stick sheets of newspaper under one edge of the tape.
- A rubber band around the bristles of a paintbrush will keep it in shape for tackling those tricky bits in corners or on a cornice. You will need replacements, because the rubber bands will deteriorate in contact with the paint.
- Push half a tennis ball over the brush handle when you are painting high areas. It will catch the drips.
- Tie plastic bags over your light fixtures when painting the ceiling above them.
- Wear a shower cap to protect your hair while you are painting the ceiling.
- If you are about to paint previously unpainted wood, rub the surface down with sandpaper and dust carefully.
- If the surface you are about to paint has already been

painted, take the extra time to wash it down first with sugar soap (available at hardware shops).

- Use wet-and-dry sandpaper to sand down each coat of undercoat. Then dust carefully.
- Sand down between coats of paint or varnish, using fine sandpaper or hardware-shop steel wool.
- When you are painting an outside wall or fence against a path, sprinkle sand on the path at your feet. Any spills can then be swept up.
- To store left-over paint without losing the top layer to time, keep it airtight by laying some aluminium foil on top of the paint (you can trace around the tin to ensure a snug fit).

PANTRY

- A pantry is an invaluable addition to a kitchen. Special pantry units can be built into kitchens. Your pantry should be in the coolest spot in the kitchen.

PARAFFIN

- Paraffin, a hydrocarbon produced from petroleum, comes in a solid form (as paraffin wax, for furniture polish) and as liquid paraffin (useful as a grease solvent). Paraffin is poisonous and flammable and must be treated with care.

PARQUET FLOORS

- Sweep regularly and clean occasionally with a damp

rather than wet mop. Excess water can get under the timber sections and cause your parquet to lift.

PARSLEY

- The best known of all herbs, parsley is a handy addition to any garden. It is grown as an annual, although you can often rely on it to resow itself for the next season.
- Unwashed parsley stored in an airtight jar has a surprisingly long life in the fridge.
- Freeze parsley when plentiful. Cut off the main stalks and place in a plastic bag. When you want to use it, simply crumble it before thawing or removing from the bag.

PASSIONFRUIT

- Passionfruit can be preserved by popping them straight into the freezer. The passionfruit will keep for up to 12 months and you'll always have 'fresh' fruit on hand.
- You can also remove the passionfruit pulp and freeze it in ice-cube trays. When frozen, take out of the trays and store in plastic bags.

PASTA

- Add a few drops of cooking oil to the water when cooking pasta, to prevent pasta pieces sticking together.

PASTRY

- Pastry is easier to make on a cold day. Make sure your hands are clean and cold too. Butter or margarine should be used straight from the fridge.
- The less water used the shorter the crust, and the less flour used in rolling out the pastry the lighter the crust.
- When covering a pie, never put pastry over hot ingredients; cool them first. Always place the pie in a preheated oven.

PATENT LEATHER

- For effective cleaning and maintenance, rub Vaseline on to your patent-leather shoes or bag and then polish it off.
- Never store patent-leather bags or shoes in plastic bags. They may sweat.

PEANUT BUTTER

- Nothing beats your own home-made peanut butter, and it is so easy to make. Simply blend some peanuts with a little peanut oil and store the mixture in a jar in your fridge. It's up to you how crunchy or smooth you make it.
- If your peanut butter has gone dry, mix in enough honey to make it spreadable again.

PEANUT OIL

- Peanut oil is a light, mono-unsaturated oil, ideal for stir-frying.

PEANUTS

- To remove skins from peanuts, place them in a hot oven for a few minutes, then plunge into cold water. The skins should come free while you are drying the peanuts.

PEARLS see JEWELLERY

PENCIL MARKS

- Remove pencil marks from clothing with an eraser or with dry-cleaning fluid. Don't attempt to remove **indelible** pencil with water (see INDELIBLE PENCIL).

PERCOLATORS

- To remove coffee stains that have built up in a percolator, place a teaspoon of powdered detergent and a teaspoon of borax together in the coffee basket, fill the percolator with hot water, and turn on. Once it has boiled, turn it off and let it stand for 10 minutes. You will then find the stains easy to brush away with a kitchen brush. Boil up a second lot of clean water, discard, and rinse well.

PEROXIDE see HYDROGEN PEROXIDE

PERSPEX

- If the cover to your perspex audio turntable is badly scratched, try polishing it with Brasso or Silvo. A small scratch can be removed by rubbing it gently and quickly with nail-polish remover.

PERSPIRATION STAINS

- Fresh perspiration stains should be sponged with undiluted ammonia. Try vinegar on old stains. Alternatively, try a biological soaker.

PETROLEUM JELLY

- Petroleum jelly (sold as Vaseline) is a semi-solid form of mineral oil, distilled from crude oil. It is useful as a household lubricant and for softening stains (see TAR).

PEWTER

- Wash your pewter in warm mild suds and polish with a soft cloth.

PHENOL see CARBOLIC ACID

PHOTOGRAPHS

- A light rub with a clean cloth and a little methylated spirits will remove finger marks from photographs.
- The most commonly used photo albums, the ones with the plastic film and adhesive pages, don't stand the test of time: the photographs can become sticky and difficult to move. By the time the baby is 10 you'll be wondering about the wisdom of putting all the baby photos in this type of album. Photographs you

are keen to preserve are best corner-mounted in an album in the old-fashioned way. But remember that colour photographs, however kindly you treat them, will not last as long as black-and-white, so think about shooting a roll of black-and-white film on that special occasion.

PIANOS

- Dust the keys regularly and wipe occasionally with a soft damp cloth. From time to time, remove the dust from the interior by using a vacuum cleaner in reverse and blowing the dust out. Don't use the top of the piano as a storage shelf and be particularly careful not to put vases or cups of coffee or drinks on the piano because a spill could cause irreparable damage.
- If you choose to leave the lid open (to make it easier for budding young musicians to practise) a strip of felt cut to fit and laid over the keys will save them from dust, and the felt hammerheads and dampers from moths.
- If the piano is to be stored, put camphor or mothballs in a cloth bag inside the piano to protect it from moths.

PICTURES

- When hanging pictures on a plasterboard wall, place a little masking tape on the wall where you want to secure the hook: it prevents the plaster from cracking, and will be hidden by the picture.

PILLOWS

- Be guided by the care label if you are planning to wash your pillows. Sponge **unwashable** pillows with a cloth wrung out in warm water and detergent.
- Fibre-filled pillows that are flattened with use can be kept plump by regular washing if you choose your day. Line-dry them in semi-shade in a warm breeze, turning frequently.

PLACE MATS

- When not in use, hang place mats from a bulldog clip on the inside of a cupboard door.

PLASTIC PANTS

- Wash frequently in very mild detergent or soap flakes after rinsing first to get rid of traces of ammonia or faeces. Dry inside out.

PLATES

- Warm dinner plates help a hot meal stay hot. Place your dinner plates in a sink of hot water, or place in a warm oven once it has been turned off. Putting cold plates in a hot oven can cause cracking and discolouring.
- Alternatively, put a little water on each plate, stack them, and microwave on HIGH for 20 seconds per plate.

PLAY DOUGH

- Play dough comes in various degrees of permanency.

Uncooked Play Dough

450 g (16 oz) white flour
225 g (8 oz) salt
water
1 tablespoon oil
food colouring

Mix together salt and flour with enough water to make a workable dough. Mix the oil through and add the colouring. Store in a plastic bag in the fridge. This has a limited life.

Cooked Play Dough

225 g (8 oz) white flour
113 g (4 oz) salt
125 ml (4 fl oz) cold water
1 tablespoon oil
2 teaspoons cream of tartar
food colouring

Stir all ingredients together and cook over a low heat for 3–5 minutes. Store in an airtight container or plastic bag. Cooked play dough lasts for months.

Play Dough

225 g (8 oz) flour
113 g (4 oz) salt
about 75 ml (2½ fl oz) water
food colouring

Mix flour and salt. Gradually add water, and food colouring if you are using it. Store in plastic until used for modelling. Then cook the clay models in a slow oven. Thin creations will take only 15–30 minutes, but thicker ones may take up to 2 hours. Paint after cooking if uncoloured.

PLAYING CARDS

- Sprinkle soiled cards with talc and place in a plastic bag. Leave for a while, shake cards in the bag, then shuffle them.

POLISH see FURNITURE POLISH, METAL POLISH, SHOE POLISH

POLISHING CLOTH

- Soak a soft clean cloth in either turpentine or paraffin, wring it out (make sure you are wearing rubber gloves!) and hang it out to dry. Use for dusting polished furniture. Do not store the cloth in a closed container.

POLISHING FLOORS

- Don't use too much polish or polish too frequently (especially in light-traffic areas), or your floor will suffer from a build-up of polish. Buff a polished floor between polishes with an electric polisher, a polishing mop, or a clean cloth tied or pinned around a broom.
- See also FLOORS.

POLYESTER

■ Polyester is made from the by-products of petrol refining; fabrics in this group include Terylene and Dacron. Polyester fabrics won't shrink or stretch and are very strong and light in weight. Wash according to instructions. Polyester fabrics can be tumble-dried.

POPLIN

■ Poplin was once 100 per cent cotton but now it can be made from cotton, viscose, silk or wool. Wash according to fibre.

PORCELAIN

■ Some cracks in fine porcelain can be scarcely noticeable if the dirt is removed from them. Drench some cottonwool in household ammonia or chlorine bleach and lay it on the crack, leaving it for several days. Keep the cottonwool moist with the solution.

PORRIDGE

■ The microwave oven has made the task of cooking porridge for one (or more for that matter) an easy one. Just place 42 g (1½ oz) oats in a breakfast bowl along with 185 ml (6½ fl oz) of water, stir and cook in the microwave for 1½ minutes on HIGH. Stir again, then cook for a further 30 seconds.

POTATOES

- To improve your potato chips, cut the potatoes and stand them in cold water for an hour before cooking. Then dry thoroughly and fry. If the chips are at all wet, the fat will spit. A pinch of salt will also prevent fat spattering.
- Peeled too many potatoes? Keep the extras in the fridge for up to 3 days by covering them with water to which a teaspoon of vinegar has been added.

POT-PLANTS

- To revive a jaded pot-plant, water with warm tea.

POTTERY

- A pottery vase may need a coating of lacquer on the inside to prevent water seeping out.

Q

QUANTITIES

- It's useful to know the measuring-spoon equivalents for weights and quantities of common cooking ingredients. See the tables at the back of this book.
- Stick a conversion table inside a kitchen-cupboard door for easy reference when you are using old recipe books.

- If you are a keen gardener, have kitchen scales in your garden shed. Quantities of fertilizer and spray often need to be weighed, and should not be taken into the kitchen because even traces of them can be harmful.

QUILTED FABRICS

- Follow the manufacturer's washing instructions. If washing in a machine, add a couple of soft towels to act as a buffer between the quilting and the machine.
- A quilt or eiderdown can be washed in a bath and then spun dry in the washing machine. The quilt can be line-dried if you distribute its weight over 3 or 4 lines and rearrange the quilt at least once during its drying.

R

RADIATORS see ELECTRIC HEATERS

RAINCOATS

- Nylon or plastic raincoats can be hand-washed in warm suds. Rinse and allow to drip-dry on a plastic coat-hanger.

RASPBERRY

- Wash a raspberry stain with sudsy water, then soak

lemon juice into the stain and leave for some time before washing out.

RATS

- If your area has rats a pet cat will earn its keep.
- Always inform your local council, and carry out their advice.

RATTLE

- Improvise a rattle for a baby by putting some rice, lentils and split peas into a clear plastic shampoo bottle with the label removed. Make sure the lid is secure by running a heated skewer around it and melting it shut permanently.

RATTLING DOORS AND WINDOWS

- A strip of foam rubber wedged around an offending door or window frame will not only silence the rattle but keep out draughts as well.

RAYON

- Rayon is a man-made fibre and comes from wood-pulp. Although it is strong when dry it is weak when wet, and care should be taken not to wring, twist or scrub wet rayon. It is best to hand-wash it frequently rather than leave it until it needs a vigorous wash.
- Iron rayon garments when they are still damp. Iron shiny rayon on the right side and matt rayon on the reverse.

RECEIPTS

- Always file receipts for major purchases. Often a warranty requires production of the receipt as well as the guarantee, and it is wise to have them at hand.

RECYCLING

- Take **aluminium cans** and **glass bottles** to a recycling point.
- **Paper** should be recycled, although recyclers may experience gluts. If you are suddenly left with a mountain of newspapers, consider some alternative uses: see NEWSPAPERS.

REFREEZING

- Don't do it. Refreezing thawed food is asking for trouble, unless, of course, you are cooking thawed food and refreezing it in a cooked state.

REFRIGERATORS

- Keep the inside of your fridge clean. Wipe up spills as soon as they occur.
- Add a little vanilla essence to the water when wiping down the inside of your fridge after defrosting it. It will smell lovely.
- See also ODOURS.

REHEATING

- Reheating food is made easy if you own a microwave.

If you are reheating a casserole, make sure the dish has enough moisture. If necessary, stir through a couple of tablespoons of extra water before reheating.

RICE

- If your rice is cooked ahead of time, place it in a colander over simmering water with foil over the top to keep hot.
- Left-over rice can be reheated in a similar manner. Add a knob of butter to the rice and cover with foil.

RIND

- Wet the grater before you grate orange or lemon rind. That way the grated rind comes off more easily. Rind can also be frozen easily, so don't automatically throw the peel of a lemon or an orange into the compost.

RINGS

- If you have a ring stuck on your finger (something that can happen easily enough during pregnancy or on a hot day), wet your finger and soap it, turning the ring as you move it over your knuckle.
- See also JEWELLERY.

ROASTING

- Roast vegetables will be cooked right through if you parboil them before roasting, or partly cook them in the microwave. Alternatively, you can complete the cooking-through of baked vegetables by giving them a short burst in the microwave before serving.

ROLLER BLINDS

- If a blind has lost its spring, remove it and rewind it in the opposite direction to the usual one. Try it a few times until you are satisfied that it has regained its old zip.

RUBBER

- Rubber marks made by furniture or shoes on kitchen floors can be removed with paraffin or mineral turpentine unless the floor is rubber. Then wipe well with sudsy water.

RUBBER GLOVES

- Rubber gloves will be easier to remove if you run your hands under the cold tap for a while before taking them off.
- Only left-hand gloves still sound? Turn some of them inside-out and use the resulting pairs for gardening.
- See also LIDS.

RUBBISH BINS see DUSTBINS

RUGS

- Mohair rugs can be machine-washed.

RUSH MATTING

- Dust collects under rush matting, so vacuum regularly if it is fixed, or vacuum under it if you can.

RUST

- Rust can be removed from most surfaces. For a stain on **fabric**, saturate with lemon juice, rub in some salt and leave for a few moments; then rinse well and wash as usual.
- On **carpet**, dab with dry-cleaning fluid, then sponge with a solution of 1 teaspoon of detergent and 1 teaspoon of white vinegar to one litre (1¾ pints) of water. If it is still visible, try lemon juice and cold water.

RUST REMOVERS AND INHIBITORS

- These preparations are available from hardware shops. Read the labels before making your choice. Follow the manufacturer's instructions.
- See also STEEL.

S

SADDLE SOAP

- Saddle soap is a special soap for cleaning leather, particularly effective in cleaning polished leathers.

SAFETY PINS

- Safety pins are handy to have in the house, and are an essential item in every first-aid kit.

SAGE

- Sage is an aromatic herb that is easily grown in the garden and will add flavour to any meat dish.

SALAD BOWLS

- Wooden salad bowls should be wiped with a damp cloth after use. Occasionally wash in warm suds, then rub some salad oil into the wood to preserve it.

SALAD DRESSING

- A quick and easy salad dressing is made as follows:

  250 ml (8 fl oz) vinegar
  375 ml (12 fl oz) olive oil
  1 teaspoon mustard
  1 teaspoon sugar

2 cloves garlic
black pepper and salt to taste

Put in a bottle or jar, shake well and store in the fridge.

SALAD GREENS

- Salad greens store best if the container, or the vegetable compartment of the fridge, is lined with a tea-towel or paper towelling. Alternatively, the greens may be washed and wrapped in a tea-towel before storing in the fridge.

SALT

- Salt may be used as an absorbent for liquid spills on **carpets**. It is particularly effective on red wine, fruit juice and urine. Apply salt generously and leave overnight before vacuuming up.
- Put a few grains of rice in the salt-shaker when filling it. Rice absorbs any moisture and prevents the holes clogging.
- Salt is the best extinguisher for a fat fire in the kitchen. Throw it on the flame. *Never* use water. (See also FAT OR OIL FIRES).

SANDPAPER

- Keep a piece of sandpaper in your kitchen drawer as well as in the toolbox. A piece of coarse sandpaper wrapped around a difficult screw-top lid will help you open it.

- Keep a sanding block or a small block of wood in the toolbox. Fold the sandpaper around this, to eliminate creases and make the job easier.

SANDWICHES

- Sandwiches freeze well, so consider making school lunches for the week all in one hit. Wrap in packages that can be doled out, and freeze. Suitable fillings for freezing include peanut butter, cheese spreads or grated cheese, ham, poultry, salmon, and tuna and mayonnaise. Extras like lettuce or tomato can be added to the lunchbox on the day.

SASHCORDS

- A broken sashcord in a window is a job for a builder. Don't take it on unless you are an experienced handyperson.

SATIN

- Satin can be made of cotton, silk, nylon, polyester or acetate. For **washable** satins, iron dry while still evenly damp, on the wrong side of the fabric. Some satins need to be dry-cleaned.

SAUCEPANS

- If the knob has come off the saucepan lid, insert a

screw from inside the lid and screw a cork down on it. It will be heatproof into the bargain.

SAUSAGES

■ Before barbecuing, prick sausages with a fork and bring to the boil or part-cook on HIGH in the microwave (3 minutes for 4 thick sausages). This will ensure that they're cooked through.

SCHOOL LUNCHES see SANDWICHES

SCISSORS

■ Like a good sharp knife, a pair of sharp scissors is a valuable tool. A good pair of scissors is best sharpened professionally from time to time. In the meantime you can sharpen them by cutting through sandpaper or steel wool.

SCONES

■ The following is a good basic recipe for scones:

250 g (8½ oz) self-raising flour
a good pinch of salt
1 teaspoon sugar
1 tablespoon butter
185 ml (6 fl oz) milk

Preheat oven to 220°C (440°F). Sift flour and salt, add sugar and rub butter into the flour, using your fingers.

Pour in milk and work lightly into a soft dough. Turn on to a floured surface and knead as lightly as you can (the less you handle the dough, the lighter the scones will be). Roll out to about 1–1.5 cm (¼–½ in) thick, stamp out with a round cutter, glaze with milk or egg yolk, and put on a hot greased oven sheet. Bake for 7–10 minutes.

SCORCH MARKS

- A solution of hydrogen peroxide and water in equal proportions may remove scorch marks, but watch it and rinse quickly when you think it has had enough.

SCRATCHES

- Light scratches on timber furniture can be concealed by rubbing with the kernel of a Brazil nut. If the timber in question is walnut, use a walnut kernel instead.

SCREWS

- Screws that are too tight or rusted in can sometimes be loosened if a drop of paraffin oil is allowed to soak in around the screw.

SEASONAL FRUIT

- It is worth buying some fruit and vegetables in bulk as they come into season. Tomatoes, for instance, tend to ripen all at once. Don't refuse them if you're offered some by a friendly gardener. It is easy to make a handy tomato sauce and freeze it for the tomato-less days ahead (see TOMATOES for recipe).

SEEDLINGS

- Cardboard egg cartons make excellent starters for seedlings. The carton section can be planted along with the seedling, since it will rot away in the garden.
- Recycle that old suitcase by transforming it into a seed bed.
- Small containers of ammonia buried among seedlings in a garden bed will keep the cats at bay.
- Store seeds in empty matchboxes, and keep in a dry place.

SEERSUCKER

- Seersucker is a lightweight crinkled summer fabric that needs no ironing. It can be made of cotton, silk, polyester or nylon.

SEMEN

- Soak stained sheets in cold water with 2 tablespoons of borax before washing as usual in the machine.

SEPTIC TANKS

- If you are staying at a house in the country, do take the trouble to find out if the toilet has a septic tank. Special care must be taken with the disposal of tampons and sanitary towels, as most septic tanks don't cope with them. Similarly, certain cleaning substances are not suitable for septic tanks, so check on the label before using on the toilet.

- 250 ml (8 fl oz) white vinegar poured into the toilet bowl and left to stand overnight is a suitable cleaner for a septic tank.

SEWING see NEEDLES

SHEEPSKINS

- Sheepskins are useful as antimacassars, floor-rugs, and for babies and invalids to lie on. Many are **machine-washable** and washing instructions will come with the article.
- When hand-washing a **non-machine-washable** sheepskin, the trick is to keep the backing as dry as possible, since it can stiffen if it gets wet. Choose your day: a warm breeze will aid drying. Vacuum the rug, then shampoo it, working the water and the wool mix (see WOOL MIX for recipe) through the fleece with your fingers. Scrape as much of the solution off the fleece as you can with your fingers and a blunt knife. Then line-hang the fleece and give it a gentle fine-spray hosing before allowing it to dry. Change its position on the line several times, making sure that you don't hang it double, or get peg marks in it.
- Dry-cleaning a sheepskin gives excellent results.

SHELVES

- Line your kitchen shelves with a waterproof paper, which can be wiped clean easily.

SHINY PATCHES

- The shiny patches on a suit or garment can be sponged with a few drops of ammonia in warm water.

SHOE BRUSHES

- Soak the brushes in warm water with detergent and a dash of household ammonia. Wash and rinse well.
- If the brushes are coated with old hardened polish, first soak the bristles in mineral turpentine. Rub out as much polish as you can on to an old cloth or newspaper, and repeat until you are satisfied with the result. Then wash and rinse.

SHOE POLISH

- Try methylated spirits to remove shoe polish from **clothing**. Dab it on gently with cottonwool, holding a clean cloth underneath the stain to prevent it from spreading.
- On **carpet**, try barely diluted wool mix (see WOOL MIX for recipe) and, if this fails, dab with dry-cleaning fluid.

SHOES

- **Leather** shoes should be cleaned and polished regularly. If they get wet, stuff them with newspaper and dry away from direct heat. Then clean and polish, and rub with a little lanolin or castor oil if the leather needs it. To ensure an even application, rub white leather shoes with a raw potato before applying your white shoe polish.

- A pump-pack spray solvent removes most of the marks from children's white **plimsolls** or **trainers**.
- New **tennis** shoes will appreciate a heavy spray with starch.
- Spray new **fabric** (denim, satin, brocade) and **canvas** or **rope-trimmed** shoes with fabric protector to help keep them looking new.

SHOWER CUBICLES

- Wipe shower screens and door **cubicles** regularly with a vinegar-soaked cloth or sponge. Bicarbonate of soda and hot water will also do the trick.
- Keep a squeegee in the shower recess so that each user can clean the surfaces quickly and easily before getting out of the shower. Most of the time you won't need any cleaning agent, because remaining traces of toilet soap and shampoo will be enough.
- See also TILES.

SHOWER CURTAINS

- Wash shower curtains (including the plastic kind) in the washing machine along with a couple of towels. Hang on the line to dry.

- If the bottom of the shower curtain has a build-up of soap, wipe it down with hot water and methylated spirits and then soak the bottom in a bucket of water and bleach for an hour or so.

SHOWER ROSES

- To remove the clogged-in lime and grime, unscrew the shower rose and clean out the head with an old toothbrush. Alternatively, you can soak the metal shower rose in vinegar overnight and attack it with the toothbrush in the vinegar the following morning.

SILK

- The finest silk comes from the larva of the mulberry-feeding silkworm *Bombyx mori*. Silk is a classic fabric equated in many minds with luxury. It should be handled with care. Discover whether your silk is washable: some silks should be dry-cleaned only.
- Never rub or scrub **washable** silks while wet. Wash after each wear because perspiration stains are very difficult to remove from silk.
- **Coloured** silks should be soaked for a few minutes after the final rinse in 3 litres (5¼ pints) of water with 2 teaspoons of vinegar; then dry without rinsing. This will negate the effect of any alkali in the detergent you used.
- Silk **stockings** will wear better if you soak them in

cold water before the first wear. After wearing, wash them in warm water and detergent. Resist the temptation to throw them into the washing machine.

SILVER

- Discover whether your silver is solid or plated. If it is plated, remember that the surface can wear off.
- Don't leave salt in your silver-plated salt-shakers if they are not in everyday use.
- Silver cutlery is quickly discoloured through daily use. Tarnish marks on spoons and the tips of forks can be removed by placing them in an old aluminium saucepan in enough cold water to cover the tarnish marks. Add 1 teaspoon of bicarbonate of soda to 500 ml (16 fl oz) water, bring it to simmering point for a few minutes, then remove cutlery and rub with a silver-polishing cloth.
- If you are the custodian of the family silver, it is probably worth buying an impregnated silver-bag to keep it in. The alternative is to wrap each piece separately in foil before putting it in a box or bag.
- Bleach will damage silver.

SILVERFISH

- Leave cloves and lavender bags among your clothes to keep them silverfish-free. Wipe your shelves down with eucalyptus or lavender oil. Silverfish don't like garlic, so some cut cloves of garlic will deter them. So will a sprinkle of Epsom salts.

SILVER-FOIL CONTAINERS

- Silver-foil containers can be recycled in various ways. Party pie containers, for example, make excellent palettes for children's poster paints.

SINKS

- To clean stainless-steel sinks, use liquid detergent on a soft cloth or sponge. Buff the sheen occasionally with an emulsion cleaner.
- Clean enamel and porcelain enamel sinks with liquid or powdered detergent. The stains that remain can be removed by soaking in household bleach.
- Enamel tends to chip, so it is worth lining the bottom of an enamel sink with a rubber mat when washing up heavy ovenproof dishes and saucepans.

SLATE

- Slate **worktops** should be sealed for best effect.
- See also FLOORS.

SLEEPING-BAGS

- Buy sleeping-bags that can be unzipped completely to make a quilt.
- A flannelette pillowcase will make a warm sleeping-

bag for a baby. Elastic threaded around the rim will keep it snugly around a baby's chest.

SLEEVE PROTECTORS

- The plastic bags that sliced bread comes in can be used to protect your sleeves during a particularly dirty job. Simply cut the ends off and use large rubber bands to hold them at your wrists.

SLIPPERS

- Felt slippers can be cleaned with carpet shampoo.

SMELLS see ODOURS

SMOKE STAINS

- Wash smoke stains off walls before painting them. Scrub with 1 part bleach to 4 parts water.

SNAILS AND SLUGS

- The greenest way to keep snails and slugs away from seedlings and new plants is to encircle plants with a magic ring of sawdust, shellgrit or sand. Neither pest likes to tackle the rough stuff.
- Another non-chemical means of control is simply to go around the garden at night once rain or watering has brought snails out in force, and pick them up.
- A saucer or can buried in the garden and filled with

beer will attract the snails. Be sure to empty it each morning.

SOAP

- Soap is biodegradable and is manufactured from animal fats or vegetable oils and caustic soda. Consider using soap powder instead of detergent in your washing machine.

SODA WATER

- Soda water is not just a good drinks mixer to have in the fridge – it also doubles as a handy carpet cleaner.

SODIUM BICARBONATE see BICARBONATE OF SODA

SODIUM CARBONATE

- Sodium carbonate is also known as washing soda, soda ash and sal soda. It is sold as a white crystalline powder or as crystals and is useful as a water softener, tarnish remover, varnish remover, for clearing drains, and for general laundry cleaning.

SODIUM CHLORIDE see SALT

SODIUM HYDROXIDE

- Sodium hydroxide is also known as sodium hydrate, caustic soda or lye. It is a very strong alkali and an ingredient in many household cleaning products. It is poisonous and can cause bad skin burns, so handle with care and keep out of reach of children.

- See also CAUSTIC SODA.

SODIUM HYPOCHLORITE

- Sodium hypochlorite may also be known as javelle water, labarraque solution, chlorine bleach or household bleach. Mix according to directions, handle with care, and avoid breathing the vapour.
- See also BLEACHES.

SODIUM PERBORATE

- Sodium perborate is a soft bleach suitable for all fabrics. Follow the manufacturer's directions. Pure sodium perborate crystals can be bought from chemists.

SODIUM TETRABORATE see BORAX

SOFT DRINKS

- Sponge a soft drink stain off clothes with a solution of 1 tablespoon of borax to 500 ml (16 fl oz) warm water.

SOFT TOYS

- When buying a soft toy for a small child it's worth paying a bit extra for a washable one. **Non-washable** soft toys can be cleaned by rubbing cornflour into the fur, then brushing briskly with a firm brush.

SOLVENTS

- A solvent is any substance that can dissolve another. Solvents useful for stain removal and household cleaning include proprietary spot-removers, methylated spirits, acetone, amyl acetate and mineral turpentine.
- Laundry solvent is often in soap-like bars and can be rubbed on shirt collars and cuffs and any stain before the garment goes into the washing machine; or it is in a spray container and can be sprayed on to the spot.

SOOT

- For a soot stain on **carpet**, vacuum by holding the tube immediately above the soot, making sure you don't rub it in further by brushing or rubbing it. Any remaining traces can be removed with carpet shampoo.

SOUP

- If you suddenly need to feed more people than you've catered for, a simple and very quick recipe for minestrone soup is to mix a can of red kidney beans (small or large), a 450-g (1-lb) can of condensed vegetable soup (made up), and 2 tablespoons of tomato paste.

SOUR CREAM

- Add a dessertspoon of white vinegar to a 300-ml (½-pint) container of cream, shake well, and – hey presto! – you have the sour cream the recipe requires.

SPAGHETTI

■ Use kitchen tongs when serving spaghetti rather than spoons or forks.

SPECTACLES

■ Clean **plastic** lenses with a *soft* cloth or tissue and a commercial cleaner or mild detergent. Clean **glass** lenses with a soft cloth moistened with a couple of drops of cloudy ammonia. Polish with a soft cloth.

■ To prevent **glass**-lensed spectacles steaming up, rub dry toilet soap on lenses and polish it off with a soft cloth.

SPIRITS

Flush stains of brandy or whisky with cold water and dab with methylated spirits. Rinse and wash the fabric as usual.

SPLINTERS

■ Remove splinters with sterilized tweezers. Grasp the end of the splinter and pull it out the same way it went in.

SPONGES see LOOFAHS

STAINED GLASS

■ Antique stained-glass windows must be wiped gently

with a damp cloth. Keep them well dusted. Modern stained glass is hardier and can be cleaned in the same way as small windowpanes.

STAINLESS STEEL

- Stainless steel is a rustproof iron alloy containing chromium. It is used extensively in cookware and tableware as well as for cutlery, kitchen sinks and bench tops.
- Clean stainless steel with hot water and detergent. It is important to dry it rather than let it drain as water spots can mark the surface.
- Be careful not to let silver dip cleaner splash on to a stainless-steel surface: the damage is permanent.
- A proprietary stainless-steel cleaner is available. This will remove heat stains, and will also remove any discolouration from eggs, mayonnaise, citrus fruits and salt.
- Don't use steel wool or other harsh scourers on your stainless-steel saucepans. Just soak in hot water before washing.

STAIN-REMOVING KIT

- Assemble a stain-removing kit and keep it handy in your laundry. Each kit should contain:

  amyl acetate (non-oily nail-polish remover)
  bicarbonate of soda
  borax

bran or talcum powder
eucalyptus oil
household ammonia
hydrogen peroxide
methylated spirits
mineral turpentine
proprietary dry-cleaning fluid
washing soda
white spirit
white vinegar

- Your usual soap and detergent should also be close to hand. You will also need clean cloths, small sponges, cottonwool, white tissues (use them only when nothing else will do), and an eye-dropper with which you can apply powerful solvents. And, with any luck, you will have a lemon in the kitchen.
- There are some easy rules to remember when removing stains:
  - Never put hot water on an unidentified stain as it may cause the stain to set.
  - Try flushing with cold water first.
  - Always use a wad of clean fabric to back the stain so that your attempts to remove it don't simply extend the stain to the next layer of material.

STAMPS

- Some stamps will peel off easily from their envelopes if left in the freezer overnight. This is worth a try before you resort to soaking them in a saucer of water.

STARCH

- Laundry starches are mostly made from cereals and are used to stiffen fabric. A well-mixed cold starch can be put into an atomizer and used as a spray starch; shake the mixture *thoroughly* immediately before spraying.

STATIC CLING

- You can rid a garment of static cling by adding (every few washes) a fabric-softener to a final rinse once all suds have been removed.
- See also LINT.

STEEL

- Unless specially treated, steel is prone to rust. Remove the rust with fine dry steel wool, then apply a rust inhibitor available from hardware shops.

STEEL WOOL

- For re-use, a steel wool pad can be stored in a jar filled with fresh soapy water. Soap pads can be put in plain water.
- Save money (and sharpen your scissors at the same time) by cutting new pads in half and using half at a time.

STEWED FRUIT

■ If you don't want your stewing fruit to disintegrate into a purée, bring the sugar and water to the boil and then add the fruit.

STICKERS see LABELS

STICKING DRAWERS

■ Cure a sticking drawer by rubbing soap or candle wax over the runners.

STICKY-BACKED PLASTIC

■ Run a hot iron over old sticky-backed plastic before removing it from shelves.

SUEDE

✿ Steel wool can remove grime from suede articles, for example, shoes, coats and bags.

SUGAR

■ Hard brown sugar can be softened by placing it for a few seconds in the microwave or in a warm oven for a few minutes.

SUNBURN

■ Be sunsmart during the summer months. Use 15+ sunscreen, a hat, and a T-shirt; and try to avoid the sun between 11 a.m. and 3 p.m.

- For the relief of mild sunburn, calamine lotion is useful. If that is unavailable, try baking soda mixed into a paste with water.

SURGICAL SPIRIT

- Surgical spirit is ethyl alcohol with the addition of castor oil and oil of wintergreen. It is used for cleaning skin.

T

TABLECLOTHS

- Treat tablecloths with fabric protector to make stains easier to wash out.
- Sew pockets into the corners of an outdoor tablecloth so that you can secure it with something weighty in breezy weather.

TABLETS

- Tablets for children can be crushed and mixed with a teaspoon (5 ml) of honey or jam to make them more palatable.

TAFFETA

- Many fibres are used to produce the lustrous stiffness

of taffeta. This effect can be lost through washing, so stick to dry-cleaning unless the washing instructions clearly recommend otherwise.

TALCUM POWDER

- Because talcum powder is highly absorbent it is a useful addition to your stain-removing kit.

TANNIN

- Remove a deposit of tannin from a silver teapot by filling the pot with a teaspoonful of borax to a litre (1¾ pints) of boiling water. Let the solution cool, then empty the pot and scrub the inside with a nylon brush. Pipe-cleaners can be used on the spout.

TAPS

- Chrome taps can be cleaned with vinegar or lemon juice. Alternatively, try a little paraffin on a damp cloth.
- See also DRIPPING TAPS.

TAR

- Soften a tar or bitumen stain by rubbing it in some petroleum jelly (Vaseline), or margarine. Then wash the fabric in the usual way.

TARRAGON

- Dried tarragon has a strong flavour. Use it sparingly.

Tarragon Vinegar

250 g (8 oz) tarragon leaves
1,250 ml (2¼ pints) white wine vinegar
sprigs of tarragon (for use at storing time)

Use tarragon leaves picked just before flowering. Wash well. Pour the white wine vinegar over the tarragon leaves. Cover and allow to stand for 3 weeks, stirring frequently. Strain the liquid and pour into sterilized bottles or jars. Put a sprig of tarragon into each container and seal. Tarragon vinegar makes an attractive gift.

TEA

- Tea stains can be treated with borax and warm water.

TEAK OIL

- Apply teak oil to the cloth, not to the wood itself. It can be used instead of polish on teak and on a number of other natural woods.

TEETHING RUSKS

- Trim crusts off bread then cut into slices 2.5 cm (1 in) thick and place on a baking tray in a slow oven for at least one hour. Store in an airtight container.

TEFLON

- Treat this non-stick coating with care, making sure

that you don't use metal spatulas or anything else that can scratch it. If you have an old Teflon-coated saucepan on which the coating has started to lift, don't use it – discard it.

- Clean non-stick surfaces with a nylon scouring pad. Most non-stick surfaces are dishwasher-safe.

TELEPHONES

- Dust your phone regularly, and occasionally use a damp cloth wrung out in detergent solution to remove odours and grime. Use a soft cloth to dry it.

TEMPERATURES

- For conversions between centigrade and fahrenheit, see the tables at the back of this book.

TERRAZZO

- Terrazzo is made of stone or marble chips and should be sealed. Both sealed and unsealed surfaces should be mopped rather than scrubbed. On a **sealed** surface, use a dash of washing-up liquid in warm water. Use 2 tablespoons of washing soda in 4 litres (7 pints) of water on an **unsealed** surface, then wipe over with a clean damp cloth mop.
- For a **worn** terrazzo surface, use 125 ml (4 fl oz) soda to 3 litres (5¼ pints) of hot water. Gently rub stains with soapy steel wool.

TERYLENE

- Treat terylene as you would treat polyester (see POLYESTER).

THAWING

- Always thaw meat completely before cooking – in your fridge if possible.

THERMOS FLASKS

- Contents of a thermos will keep hot longer if the flask has been pre-heated with boiling water.
- If your flask smells of tea or coffee, put 2 tablespoons of bicarbonate of soda and 500 ml (¾ pint) boiling water into the flask. Give it a good shake and leave it for about 10 minutes, then pour out and rinse with boiling water.
- To rid your thermos of a musty smell, three-quarters fill with boiling water to which you have added a tablespoon (15 ml) of sugar. Shake well and leave for about half an hour. Then empty and rinse with fresh water.
- Between uses, always store a thermos flask with the lid off.

THRIP see APHIDS

THYME

- Garden thyme can be grown in your garden and picked throughout the year for use fresh in cooking. It has a warm, aromatic and slightly pungent flavour, stronger when dried. Use thyme leaves in soups and stuffings, with fish, beef, chicken, veal and strongly flavoured vegetables. Thyme combines well with sage and marjoram.

- Harvest the plants just before they start to flower and hang in bunches in a shady spot. When they are brittle and dry, take off the leaves and store them in airtight containers.

TIGHTS

- Net bags are available at many supermarkets to make washing your tights and stockings easy. Simply place them in the bag and put it into an appropriate machine-wash. Alternatively, put them in a sock secured with a rubber band.
- Old tights have numerous uses. Here are a few:
  - hanging jumpers on the clothes-line;
  - cleaning surfaces that need gentle handling;
  - ties for garden plants;
  - protecting ripening fruit from birds;
  - storing apples or onions in your garden shed.

TILES

- Clean ceramic tiles with methylated spirits (keep the area ventilated), or mineral turpentine if they are greasy. Rinse kitchen tiles thoroughly after cleaning.
- See also SHOWER RECESS.

TOFFEE APPLES

- Try this easy recipe:

500 g (17 oz) sugar
250 ml (8 fl oz) cold water
2 tablespoons vinegar
12 small red eating apples
12 sturdy wooden skewers

Boil sugar, water and vinegar in a saucepan until a spoonful of mixture cracks when placed in cold water. Stand pan in a sink of hot water. Skewer apples and dip them in the hot syrup to cover. Stand toffee apples to dry on greased trays.

TOILETS

- Wipe down the seat, lid and surrounds daily.
- The best way to clean the toilet bowl is with a toilet brush and a lot of elbow grease. However, there are many toilet cleaners on the market; using them may make you feel the toilet is even cleaner. Don't forget to clean under the rim.
- Don't mix your toilet cleaners, because they can combine to produce noxious and explosive gases. Some are unsuitable for use in septic tanks, so check the container.
- The choice for the environment is white vinegar.

TOMATOES

- Tomatoes are easily peeled if you dunk them for a couple of minutes in boiling water.
- This handy tomato sauce for pasta is easy to make:

  olive oil for frying
  1 onion, sliced
  6 tomatoes
  oregano
  salt and pepper to taste
  1 tablespoon tomato paste
  250 ml (8 fl oz) warm water

  Heat olive oil in a frying pan, add onion and allow to brown. Add the tomatoes, mashing them into the hot oil. Add oregano, salt and pepper. Dissolve tomato paste in the warm water. Add to the sauce and stir. May be frozen for later use.
- Freeze unused tomato paste in an ice-cube tray.

TOOTHBRUSHES

- Don't toss out old toothbrushes. They are invaluable cleaning aids because they can reach into all sorts of nooks and crannies large brushes can't.

TOOTHPASTE

- For a stain on fabric, gently scrape off any solid matter and sponge or flush out the rest with plain water.

TORTOISESHELL

- Rub in olive oil or Vaseline with a soft cloth.

TOWELS

- Towels that don't really absorb moisture can be improved by soaking overnight in water to which borax has been added.

TRAINERS

- Many of today's trainers can be thrown into the washing machine with the weekly wash (depending on just how dirty they are, of course!). Dry in the sun if possible, or else over a heating vent or within range, but not right in front of, a radiator.

TULLE

- Tulle is a fine net fabric made in various fibres. Some don't wash well, so try to choose the synthetic, more easily washable types for children's costumes. Restiffen limp tulle with weak hot-water starch.

TUMBLE-DRYER

- Tumble-dryers are a boon to mothers of nappy-wearing infants during wet weather – but save energy by using the clothes-line when you can.
- Never tumble-dry woollens, and follow the instructions when tumble-drying acrylics.
- A number of fabrics object to being tumble-dried for

long on a high setting, so check regularly and keep drying time to a minimum.

- A dry towel placed in the dryer will help cut down on drying time.

TURMERIC

- Turmeric is a yellow spice that can be added to rice when it is cooking, and is used in curries.
- See also CURRY.

TURPENTINE

- Don't store mineral turpentine in a plastic container: it can dissolve some plastics. Keep the tin you buy the first lot in, and have it refilled.

TWEED

- Dry-clean new tweed garments. Wash old tweed garments in a wool mix (see WOOL MIX), spin very briefly, and hang on a coat-hanger to dry.

U

UMBRELLAS

- Never store a damp umbrella. Open it and allow it to dry before putting it away. A black umbrella that looks dull will benefit from a sponging with cold water and vinegar.

UNBLEACHED CALICO

- In the first wash of unbleached calico, add white spirit to lighten the fabric and get rid of the starch.
- Drying in the sun will gradually bleach the fabric.

UPHOLSTERY

- Upholstered furniture is always in fashion, but care requirements vary. Make sure that you get cleaning instructions with any new purchases. Discover whether your upholstery fabric has been treated to make it stain-resistant; otherwise, consider treating it yourself (with Scotchguard, for example). Regular vacuum-cleaning is an important part of maintenance.
- See also LEATHER UPHOLSTERY.

URINE

- For cat or dog urine on **carpet**, sponge the stain with white vinegar, then wash the area with wool mix (see WOOL MIX for recipe). Dry as you go with a rough towel.
- For human urine on **fabric**, mop up the stain with salt, then flush with cold water. Treat any remaining stain with neat household ammonia. On **carpet**, sponge immediately with cold water, then mop with equal parts of white vinegar and cold water. Rinse, then blot dry.

V

VACUUM CLEANERS

■ A good vacuum cleaner will make your cleaning tasks much easier. When buying a cleaner, look for one that is comfortable to use, and consider the *kinds* of surfaces you will be cleaning. A small, light cleaner (perhaps battery-operated) may be a convenient addition for quick clean-up jobs.

VACUUM FLASKS see THERMOS FLASKS

VALUABLES

■ Often you don't know what you've got until it's gone, as the song goes. Don't under-estimate your sentimental attachment to possessions, and make sure you keep them safe. It is worth having jewellery valued, and keeping a list and photographs of pieces. Consider using a safe deposit.

VARNISH

❧ To clean old-fashioned varnished surfaces, mix equal parts of raw linseed oil and paraffin and apply with a clean cloth.

VASELINE

❧ On **fabric**, scrape off as much of the Vaseline as

you can, then treat the spot with dry-cleaning fluid.

- Vaseline can be removed from **carpet** with a little paraffin. Then treat with dry-cleaning fluid before sponging with warm water and detergent.
- See also PETROLEUM JELLY.

VASES

- A handful of pebbles or marbles in the bottom of a light-weight vase will keep it upright.

VEGETABLE OILS

- Vegetable oils are invaluable in cooking. Useful oils to have on your shelves are peanut oil (it is flavourless) and olive oil (for dishes requiring its distinctive flavour).

VEGETABLE STAINS

- Most vegetable stains on fabric can be removed by treating with borax and water: 2 tablespoons of borax dissolved in 1 litre (1¾ pints) of warm water.

VELOUR

- Velour is a fabric with a heavy pile, usually acrylic. Follow the manufacturer's washing instructions.

VELVET

- Velvet fabric may be silk, cotton or synthetic. Follow the manufacturer's instructions in caring for velvet.

- Special stain-resisters are available for protecting velvet **upholstery**.
- To restore the crushed pile of a velvet **garment**, steam it over a boiling kettle or hang it in the bathroom while you are taking a shower.

VELVETEEN

- New velveteen and corduroy garments often shed dye, so wash separately for the first couple of washes.
- You can set dark dyes by soaking the garment for half an hour in 2 litres (3½ pints) of cold water to which a (8¾-pint) bucket of warm water makes a good wall wash as usual.
- Most corduroy and velveteen garments don't require ironing. Smooth the pile with your hand when you hang the garment on the line.

VENEERED WOOD

- Mop up any spills immediately, or the damp may lift the veneer. Dust with care.

VENETIAN BLINDS

- To clean, wear a pair of cotton gloves, or hold a soft clean cloth, and run the slats between your fingers and thumb.

VINEGAR see ACETIC ACID

VINYL FLOORS

- A large range of vinyl flooring is available and one of the advantages it has over other surfaces is its ease of cleaning. Ask your retailer about the maintenance of the flooring you choose.
- Rubber and some shoe heels may mark vinyl. Don't use anything drastic in attempting to remove these marks – some washing-up detergent on steel wool and a *gentle* rubbing will remove most.
- A shiny vinyl surface will shine even more if you add a tablespoon of fabric-softener to the washing water.

VINYL UPHOLSTERY

- Wash occasionally with a soft cloth and sudsy water.
- See also BALLPOINT PEN.

VISCOSE

- Viscose is a man-made fibre produced from wood-pulp. It can be made to look like just about anything, including silk, wool, linen or cotton. It is weak when wet, so handle carefully when washing: don't wring or twist it.

VIYELLA

- Viyella is a brand name for a fine, light, warm fabric woven from wool and cotton. Hand-wash gently in warm water.

VOMIT

- For **washable** fabrics, remove as much as possible of the solid matter with a spatula and then pre-rinse. Washing in a solution of water and wool mix (see WOOL MIX for recipe) will not only remove the stain but should get rid of the smell as well.
- On **carpet** or **mattress**, remove solid matter with a spatula and use an old towel or bath mat to blot up as much moisture as possible. Sponge the area with a solution of 250 ml (8 fl oz) water to 1 tablespoon of liquid laundry detergent and 1 tablespoon of white vinegar. Be careful not to get the area too wet. Blot dry as you go, and use dry-cleaning fluid to remove any remaining grease content.

W

WALLPAPERING

- To remove old wallpaper, use equal parts of vinegar and hot water and a paint roller or sponge to drench the paper. Do this twice. The wet paper should peel off easily.
- When patching wallpaper, hide the joins by cutting around the pattern or extending the patch to an inconspicuous point, for example, a room corner.

WALLS

- 125 ml (4 fl oz) ammonia, 60 ml (2 fl oz) white vinegar and a tablespoon of washing soda added to a 5-litre (9½ pints) bucket of warm water makes a good wall cleaner for everyday use. Sugar soap (available at hardware shops) is another cheap and effective wall cleaner if you are planning to paint or wallpaper.
- So you've changed your mind about where that painting should go. Nail holes can be hidden from view on white walls with a little white toothpaste.

WALNUTS

- To remove walnuts whole from their shells, either soak them overnight in salted water or put them in a moderate oven for about 15 minutes.
- Walnuts are handy when removing small scratches from walnut furniture. Simply rub the scratch with a cut surface.

WASHING BLUE

- Remember the old laundry blue-bags? The water-soluble blue dye is still available in bag form, and liquid blues are available from supermarkets. A tiny bit of blue makes yellowing cottons look white; but be cautious with synthetics, or they may look grey.

WASHING MACHINES

- Don't overload or underload your washing machine.

Use slightly less detergent than the manufacturer suggests and try to choose a detergent which is environmentally friendly.

- Keep the inside of the machine clean by once in a while pouring 500 ml (15 fl oz) vinegar into it and putting it on WASH.

WASHING SODA see SODIUM CARBONATE

WASPS

- The wasp is a most unwelcome guest at many a picnic or barbecue. Unlike the bee, the wasp can sting repeatedly. The sting can be dangerous.
- If you see a large number of wasps, you may have a wasp nest. Notify your local council and they will advise you what to do.
- Don't serve soft drink in cans if there are wasps about: they can slip into the can and sting the back of the throat, causing swelling that can make breathing impossible.
- Clean up all remains of food and drink immediately.
- Chemical-free wasp traps have been devised. The wasp is lured into a container by a sweet wine and will drown itself because it can't escape.
- In severe cases of stings, don't hesitate to call an ambulance. With single stings, a solution of baking powder or a cut onion may relieve the pain.

WASTE DISPOSAL UNITS

- Remove any unpleasant odours by grinding orange rinds, or half a lemon.

WATER

- Water is always the first option when it comes to stain removal. Stick to cold water first for any non-greasy stain.
- Most water supplies have some additives these days, the most common one being fluoride. Water filters are available through most health food shops and plumbing suppliers. Once you taste the difference you may want a purifier installed.

WATERCOLOUR PAINT

- Flush with cold water and treat the remaining stain with neat household ammonia on the wet fabric. Rinse well.

WATERPROOFING

- Silicone water-repellents are available from hardware shops and camping shops. You can use them to waterproof your camping gear, ski clothes and whatever else you want to keep dry.

WATER-SOFTENERS

- Various areas in England suffer from hard water. Use a commercial product according to the instructions on the packet. Washing soda and borax are also effective water-softeners.

WEEVILS see BAY LEAVES

WHITE SPIRIT

- White spirit is a clear solvent made from mineral oils. It is useful to have on hand in a stain-removing kit, but treat it with care: it is flammable and toxic.

WINDOW BOXES

- When adding soil to window boxes, line the base of the box with a newspaper or two. The paper will prevent the soil from drying out too quickly.

WINDOWS

- Don't wash your windows with soap. Use 125 ml (4 fl oz) ammonia, 125 ml (4 fl oz) white vinegar and 2 tablespoons of cornflour to a bucket of water. A cool, calm day gives you a better chance of polishing them before they dry in streaks.
- Shine windows with old newspapers rather than paper towels: it is cheaper, greener, and paper towels sometimes leave bits behind.
- Alternatively, wash, scrub and dry with a squeegee dipped in water and detergent. This method is quick and efficient.
- Don't use abrasive pads on glass. Remove paint and

other hard material with a blade-scraper (available at hardware shops): it never scratches.

- When washing the **inside** of your windows, drape your curtains over a coat-hanger and hang it from the curtain rail. It will keep them well out of the way.
- The **outsides** of your windows can be cleaned with a long-handled mop, rinsed with a hose, and left to dry.

WINE

- For red wine on **clothing** or a **tablecloth**, mop up the excess with paper towels and use soda water, being careful not to spread the stain further. Alternatively, smother with salt and leave for several hours. For red wine on **carpet**, use a white cloth or white paper towels to mop up the excess, and dab – don't wipe. Then smother the stain completely with salt, talc or some absorbent powder. Leave it overnight and vacuum the next day.
- A white wine stain will respond to soda water if caught early.

WOOL

- The versatility of wool has increased and machine-washable woollen garments are readily available. Hand-washing is still the most suitable method for many woollen jumpers, and if you use a wool mix (see below) you can omit a rinse. Proprietary wool-wash preparations are also recommended.

WOOL MIX

- Here is a home-made wool mix that keeps indefinitely:

  250 ml (8 fl oz) methylated spirits
  1 small packet Lux or Dreft flakes
  1 small bottle eucalyptus oil

  Mix together. Use 1 tablespoon (15 ml) to a bowl of water. Garments need not be rinsed when washed with wool mix.

WORK CLOTHES see OVERALLS

WORK TOPS

- Food-preparation areas should be wiped down after every use to avoid the transfer of bacteria from raw to cooked food.

WROUGHT IRON

- Wipe wrought iron clean with a cloth wrung out in detergent suds. Rust spots can be removed with steel wool dipped in liquid paraffin.

X, Y, Z

XEROX POWDER

- The inking powder from a photocopier should come out with a brisk brushing. Make sure it doesn't get wet.

YOGHURT

- Natural (plain) yoghurt is a good substitute for cream in mashed potatoes, makes a handy and quick dessert with fruit, and is useful for curries and some soups. It is also delicious mixed in equal proportions with ice-cream.

ZINC CREAM

- Neat wool mix (see WOOL MIX for recipe) will remove zinc cream from most **washable** fabrics.

ZIPPERS

- Try rubbing soap on to a jammed zipper. Talcum powder and lead pencil are also both tried-and-true methods for keeping zippers working smoothly. Close zippers before washing garments.

CONVERSION TABLES

Weight

Metric	Imperial
25 g	1 oz
50 g	2 oz
75 g	2½ oz
100 g	3½ oz
125 g	4½ oz
150 g	5½ oz
175 g	6½ oz
200 g	7 oz
225 g	8 oz
250 g	8½ oz
300 g	10½ oz
450 g	16 oz (1 lb)
500 g	1⅛ lb
750 g	1¾ lb
1,000 g (1 kg)	2¼ lb
2 kg	4½ lb

Volume

Standard	Metric	Imperial
1 teaspoon	5 ml	
1 tablespoon	15 ml	½ fl oz
1½ tablespoons	22 ml	1 fl oz
2 tablespoons	30 ml	
2½ tablespoons	37 ml	1½ fl oz
½ litre	500 ml	¾ pint
1 litre	1,000 ml	1¾ pints
1½ litres	1,500 ml	2½ pints
2 litres	2,000 ml	3½ pints

Oven Temperatures

	Electric		Gas	
	°C	°F	°C	°F
Low or cool	95	200	95	200
Very slow	120	250	120	250
Slow or warm	150	300	150–160	300–325
Moderately slow	160	325	160–175	325–350
Moderate	175	350	175–190	350–375
Moderately hot	190	375	190–205	375–400
Hot	205	400	205–230	400–450
Very hot	230	450	230–260	450–500

OTHER TITLES IN THE SERIES

Tips and Techniques for Microwave Cooking
Family First Aid
How to Make Over 200 Cocktails
Choosing Baby Names
Chess Made Easy
Transform Your Public Speaking
Choosing Dog Names
Choosing Cat Names
The Pocket Easy Speller